THE CHURCH IN CHAINS

THE CHURCH IN CHAINS

by

Richard Wurmbrand

HODDER AND STOUGHTON
London Sydney Auckland Toronto

CONTENTS

'There is no better rest in this restless world than to face imminent peril of death solely for the love and service of God our Lord.'

St. Francis Xavier

CHAPTER 1

Episodes in the Life of the Underground Church

In North Korea few workers have a free day. They work from the 1st of January to the 31st of December. The revolutionary feasts are celebrated by increased production. You can stay at home only when you are sick.

In a big coal-compound with some 40,000 workers, it was observed that 1,200 always reported sick on Sundays. The authorities became suspicious, and they discovered that, in turns, these gathered in private homes or, during the good season, in the woods. Their pastor would announce a hymn, but nobody would sing. The danger of being heard was too great. They all would read silently at the same time the respective songs from hymnals written by hand. Then they would pray, also in perfect silence. The pastor would read a few Bible verses and give a very short exhortation—meditated upon in silence by the whole congregation, which would disband afterwards in small groups, looking around to be sure that nobody saw them.

Forty-five Christians considered to be leaders of this Christian group have been shot. We do not know the fate of others.

What is this? A scene in the life of the Underground Church. It happened in 1969.

Rev. Fang-Cheng is in jail. He has been tortured, but has not betrayed the brethren.

One day he is brought again before the examining officer. He sees in a corner of the room a heap of rags, and hears a rattling of chains. The image becomes clearer. It is his mother. But she did not have white hairs before. Now she has. The colour of her face is like ashes. You can see that she, too, has passed through heavy ordeals.

The Communist says to Cheng, 'I have heard that you Christians have ten commandments allegedly given by God, which you strive to fulfil. I would be interested to know them. Would you be so kind as to recite the commandments?'

Cheng is in a terrible state of heart, but still such an opportunity to acquaint a disciple of Mao with God's law must not be neglected. He begins to enumerate the commandments until he arrives at 'Honour father and mother'. Here he is interrupted. The Communist tells him, 'Cheng, I wish to give you the opportunity to honour your mother. Here she is, suffering and in chains. Tell us what you know about your brethren in faith and I promise that tonight you and your mother will be free. You will be able to give her care and honour. Let me see now whether you really believe in God and wish to fulfil his commandment.'

It is not easy to take a decision.

Cheng turns to his mother—'Mummy, what shall I do?' The mother answers, 'I have taught you from childhood to love Christ and his holy Church. Don't mind my suffering. Seek to remain faithful to the

Saviour and his little brethren. If you betray them, you are no more my son.'

This was the last time that Fang-Cheng saw his mother. The probability is that she died under torture.

What is this? A scene from the life of the Underground Church.

An officer of the Secret Police sits in the study of a pastor. The Communist is very polite. He asks the pastor to become an informer for the Secret Police. In exchange, he can preach as much as he likes. 'And then, you know, we have a voice in the Church today. We can help to make you a bishop.'

The pastor refuses.

It is a Saturday afternoon. The Communist leaves. When he is already at the door, he says, 'I will be back for a definite answer on Monday. You had better think it over. By the way, your congregation considers you a saint. But you remember your affair with Betty. It went far. We have a picture of her in your embrace. You have been very incautious. If your congregation knew the story, you would be finished. I wish you well! Better accept our proposal. In any case, goodbye, and have a very blessed Sunday.'

On Sunday morning the pastor tells from the pulpit his love affair, omitting only the name of the girl. He says, 'We all are sinners, pastors as much as laymen. I have failed. The Secret Police is blackmailing me, but I would rather, in shame, confess my sin to you than consent to inform against you. God forgives, and I will not become a Judas. The wrong which I have done is enough. For the rest, it is up to you to decide if I can stay on as your pastor or not.'

When he descends from the pulpit, the parishioners throng around him. In tears they kiss him and say,

'Don't leave us. We are not better than you. Now you will be the best of pastors.'

When the Communist comes back on Monday, the pastor says, 'Just go ahead and publish what I have done.' The publishing does not discredit him. Everyone answers, 'We know the story. He has told us himself, and we forgave him.'

Soon after this, the pastor is sent to prison, but it is like going to a feast.

What is this? A scene from the life of the Underground Church.

A Christian has been released from prison. He is a farmer. He goes into the fields and prays, 'God make me perfect.' An inner voice answers, 'Would you be ready to return to prison in order to become perfect?' He shrinks back. He has suffered so much. He replies, 'Anything else, God, only not this.' The inner voice says, 'Then do not ask to be perfect.'

A long inner struggle follows. In the end the Christian yields. 'Make me perfect at whatever cost,' he prays. Soon he is re-arrested and put in solitary confinement. He passes a long term there. Beatings, hunger, lack of sun, no reading material. His only pastime is to communicate by Morse code through the wall with his fellow-prisoners. One day he has near him a new prisoner. He asks him his name. It is the same as his own. It is his son. Encouraged by the heroic example of the father, the son has also walked the way of the cross and has also arrived in jail. The father thanks God for the privilege given him to have a confessor of the faith as a son. A remarkable step on the way to perfection.

What is this? An occurrence from the life of the Underground Church, as reported in *Vestnik Spasenia*

(The Herald of Salvation), the secret magazine of the Russian Baptists.

Sovietskaia Bielorussia of the 15th of August 1967 said, 'Ignorant fanatics of the Utevsk Baptist Evangelical Christian Church have woven their nest in the area. . . They are determined to convert the population and to establish the rule of the evangelical ideology over the land, to introduce religious instruction of children and the abolishment of anti-religious propaganda. They urge each person to earn their salvation by active recruitment and winning others to Christ.'

The Moscow publishing house Znanie published recently a book by a Communist A. Shamaro, called *Irreconcilability*. It thunders against the Christians. But at the same time it describes them: 'The preachers, the active bearers of religion in all its forms—in churches or sects?—don't laugh and don't make jokes. They act. They work day and night. They preach everywhere, at bus-stations and in hospital wards. They seek new men for the parishes or sectarian congregations. They seek them everywhere. They would stop on the streets unknown men whom they saw to have a sad face. . . Day and night they seek the sheep that have gone astray. "Faith without works is dead", they say. And the first work pleasant to God and which honours him . . . they consider to be "the fishing of men", the attraction of new adherents in church parishes and sectarian groups. . . If the dirty religious preachers and recruiters endeavour not to miss any occasion to fish a soul among those with whom they work, with whom they live in the same town or village, with whom they meet on the street, they surely do everything to fill with religious faith the heads of their children, and of the children belonging to relatives and acquaintances.'

Where are there such faithful pastors? Where are these zealous Christians? We do not meet them often in the free world. You have heard again about the Underground Church, as described by her worst enemies.

A letter arrives. The writer introduces himself as a florist. He is a specialist in growing orchids. He has cultivated new varieties of orchids which can grow even in Northern Siberia. From those parts, and also from many other parts of the country, people come to copy his catalogue of twenty-seven new kinds of orchids. (By the way, what a coincidence! The New Testament is composed of twenty-seven books. Could it be that he is the lucky possessor of a New Testament and that people come to copy it by hand?) He says that the most appreciated are his Amosian orchids, types 8 and 11. I open the Bible at Amos 8:11 and read 'Behold, the days come, says the Lord God, that I will send a famine in the land, not a famine of bread, nor a thirst for water, but of hearing the words of the Lord.'

In this shrewd manner, this brother informs western Christians about the urgent need for more Bibles.

Others make it simpler. A Christian begins his letter with the words 'Dear Censor, I know that every letter written abroad is censored. But you are also a man created by God, who will stand one day before his judgement seat. Allow this letter to pass. It does not harm the state. I simply communicate with my brethren in faith in another country.' The letter passed. Some Communist censors are also men with hearts.

A tourist returns from the Soviet Union. She received there various little gifts, among them a towel. The tourist is thoroughly searched when she leaves the U.S.S.R., but nobody pays attention to the towel.

When we get it, we dip it in a chemical solution. And we can read a communication from the Underground Church.

There exists a church which keeps relationship with other churches by methods like this.

Mrs. Ghinzburg is a Soviet writer and a Communist. Notwithstanding, she has been in Soviet prisons some seventeen years. She has been jailed by her own Party comrades. This is not an exceptional case. Communism is not only anti-Christian, or anti-Jewish, or anti-imperialist. It is simply anti-everybody. One Communist hates another Communist. The Communist Kosygin put manacles on the wrists of the Communist Dubcek. Mao hates Kosygin. Kosygin hates Tito. Krushchev kept his own wife in prison eight years. It is a religion of hatred. In Party purges, thousands of Communists have been jailed and killed. Mrs. Ghinzburg has been one of the victims.

Released from prison, she wrote a book called *The Whirlwind*. She asserts that she still has Communist convictions. Nevertheless, she describes honestly the horrors of Communist prison-camps. Among other things, she says that in the north of Siberia, where the snow never melts, some Christian women prisoners refused to work on Easter Sunday, saying that they had to celebrate the Lord's resurrection. They were punished by being made to stand barefoot on the ice. And the Communist writer adds, 'Not one of them fell sick.'

It reminds us of what happened 1,600 years ago.

Forty Christian officers serving in a Roman legion in Sebaste (Armenia), refused to bring a sacrifice to the Roman Emperor, as to a god. They were stripped naked and made to stand on the ice of the river Kisil-Irmak. On the shore, a fire burned. A warm bath was prepared for those who would recant. Every hour they were asked if they were ready to renounce their faith, in which case their life would be spared. In the end, one denied the Saviour. At that moment the Roman centurion, who watched the execution, saw forty angels with forty crowns descending from heaven to crown the martyrs. But one of the angels found no head on which to put his crown. The would-be martyr had become a renegade. So the centurion stripped himself of his clothes, and crying, 'Angel, I come,' ran to the ice. He died, as did the others, for the glory of the Saviour.

Those have died. The sisters in Siberia did not die. But neither was there even one who recanted.

This is the Underground Church as described by a Communist writer.

The Christian Ketchik had been converted late in life. He lived on a small pension. His wife did not share his Christian faith.

One day, Ketchik was found at a secret prayer-meeting and compelled to pay, as a fine, his income for two months. He came back from court happy, and told his wife, 'Now you see that I was right telling you the great worth of prayer. You did not believe me. But look here —the sentence. The Communists know the value of prayer. Even in their eyes a prayer has the value of two months' pension. If it is of such high price, from now on I will never miss a prayer-meeting.' He was fined three times during one year. He lost his income for half a year. But he learned the truth of what St. Augustine said: 'Prayer is the strength of Christians and the weakness of God.'

This is another of the many happenings in the life of the Underground Church.

Monsignor Draganovic was head of the Yugoslavian section at the Vatican. He himself is a Croatian.

But then the Vatican decided to arrive at an understanding with Tito. He had not killed all the Catholics. You just pass over the corpses of the hundreds of thousands dead, forget to mention their innocent death any more, and you sign a concordat. So Monsignor Draganovic, opponent of Communism, had to leave the Vatican. But he continued to work from Germany on behalf of his persecuted brethren.

He foresaw the possibility that he might be kidnapped. Therefore he wrote and deposited in a safe place a statement that he had no intention of returning to Yugoslavia of his own free will. Should any contrary statement appear later, then friends would know that he had been the victim of a plot. Monsignor Draganovic was lured to Trieste where allegedly one waited for him to give him more documents and pictures about Tito's crimes. From Trieste he disappeared.

The foreign correspondents in Belgrade were shown afterwards a declaration written by Draganovic in which he stated that he returned to his fatherland of his own choice. The reporters even received photocopies of the document. It was certainly his handwriting. But Monsignor Draganovic was a sophisticated writer. In this declaration the syntax was that of an illiterate. It had been dictated by a Communist officer of little education.

After a few weeks Draganovic himself appeared before the foreign press, and declared that he had decided to come back to Yugoslavia to stand trial under the charge of having been a 'war criminal', though he had never been in the army. Only God knows through what methods of torture and brainwashing he had passed before giving such a declaration.

The American Government apologised to the North Korean Communists for having intruded into territorial waters, though it had not been true. This happened even though the American president had not been beaten by the Communists. Why should we wonder about Draganovic?

This bishop did not resist. Nobody must misjudge him. Two hundred pounds of flesh under Communist torture is not a man. It has ceased to be a human body.

Under a Communist whip, tortured flesh may reveal a hero, a traitor, or a weakling.

Christians meet in a wood. The police surround them. Several try to flee, but they are caught by dogs.

Many get short terms of prison, fifteen days, but they have to pay for their board in the hospitable institution which detains them! A heavy burden for a family of poor Soviet citizens.

A Christian lady fights with the policemen. She would not allow her hymnal to be taken away from her. She has had it for forty years and could not replace it. She bleeds. Her nose is broken. She also has injuries to her arms. Just visualise the scene. Physical violence endured for possessing a book containing praises to God, while we have hymnals and never sing except in church.

In the U.S.S.R., hundreds of families have their children taken away because they teach them the Christian faith. Now, these families understand in a new manner the words of the Lord, 'Except ye become as children, ye cannot enter the Kingdom of Heaven.' According to them this means unless you accept to become sufferers like these children, unless you accept to lose the one most beloved as they lose their mummies and daddies, there is no place for you in the Kingdom.

This is a new interpretation of the Bible, or rather a return to an old interpretation, and it happens in this world apart, the world of the Underground Church.

Children fight. The teacher says, 'Cosmonauts have been in space and have not met God.' A pupil stands up. The child knows that by its Christian witness it may lose father and mother. But she says, 'Comrade teacher, did the astronauts have a pure heart? Without it you will never see God on whatever star you arrive. If you have it, you can see God everywhere, even while sitting on a form in an atheistic school.'

In another school, the children are taught that man comes from a monkey. The teacher, suspecting Eve to be a Christian girl, points at her and asks her what she thinks about it. She answers, 'I am thankful, comrade teacher, for what you taught us today. I have always asked myself how it is that Communists are so wicked and torture so many innocent men. Now you have given me the explanation. You are from the monkeys.'

The children Vania, Pavlik, Andrei, Vera and Sveta were given a rubber doll. When the children played 'a prayer-meeting', they were embarrassed by the fact that the knees of the doll could not be bent. So they complained to the teacher that they have an unbelieving doll. 'We have learned that every knee must bow before the Name of Jesus.' What a lesson for an atheist!

Many children taught in the Underground Church say openly what they think about God, and also what they think about Communists.

Y. I. Kushev stands before a court in Moscow. He has been one of the organisers of a demonstration on a public square against the arrest of Soviet writers. He had shouted, 'Release Dobrovolski. Down with dictatorship.'

The prosecutor asks him, 'Do you believe in God? — Yes.'

Then Anatalovy Krasnov-Levitin takes the stand as witness for the defence. He had brought Kushev to Christ. Doing this he knows that he exposes himself to heavy sufferings. Krasnov-Levitin had already been for seven years in prison for his Orthodox faith. Now he sees his convert in the dock. It is not like bringing somebody to Christ and then rejoicing that he sings dressed in a choir-robe in the church.

Krasnov-Levitin says, 'It is under my influence that Kushev asked to be baptised. I was on the square. Someone said to me, "They've arrested Kushev." I ran after him, but it was too late. They pushed him into a car and drove off. And now I see him after eight months —here, pale and drawn after his long imprisonment . . . he is a man of exceptional integrity . . . What happened to him is the direct result of his generosity . . . he is very unselfish, always thinking of others, never of himself. A gifted poet . . . he has all the makings of a brilliant writer.'

The defence asks, 'Were you pleased to have him baptised?' Levitin: 'Of course I was pleased. What kind of a religious man or writer would I be if I wasn't happy when people come to believe in God? But I am most displeased to see him in court.' The defence (which in the Soviet Union also acts as the prosecution): 'You think you can baptise a nineteen year old boy without his parents' knowledge?'— 'There is a canonical rule that the church is not entitled to refuse baptism to anyone, and the Gospels call upon everyone without exception to be baptised.'

The lawyer Alski 'defending' Kushev: 'Levitin asserted his right to be religious and to propagate religion; but no one has given him the right to subvert minors to religion or to use compulsion. In coming to your verdict, I ask you to keep in mind the need to protect such youngsters from Levitin.'

Soon after the trial of Kushev, Levitin was also arrested. A Communist, general-major P. Grigorenko, protested against the injustices. He is an atheist, but Levitin called him 'the good Samaritan' who helps, while priests pass by. Grigorenko has been interned in an asylum.

A new fashion appeared in the Russian town of Liubetz. Women wore ribbons with inscriptions like, 'May God arise and His enemies be dismayed', 'The Most High is alive to help', 'May the devils perish before the face of the living God', and so on. These were worn publicly in open defiance of the Communists.

But how could they be produced? Every factory has a political commissar who surveys everything. Well, it so happened that the man the Secret Police appointed for the textile factory of Liubetz was a secret Christian. He had infiltrated the police in order to help the cause of Christ. His name is Stasiuk. He has been discovered and is in prison now. But he did it.

This is how the Underground Church works.

Some of the Underground Churches, especially those from among the Orthodox, are also politically active. Christians would like not to be busy in politics. But when Communists are busy meddling in church affairs, and killing or imprisoning millions of Christians, believers have not much choice. They have to defend themselves. Did not the Scottish Covenanters fight with weapons against bloody King James II?

In Leningrad, a plot to overthrow the Communist regime—planned by brethren of the Orthodox Underground Church—has been discovered. Involved in it were sixty intellectuals of high-rank position.

On this occasion we received the explanation as to how it was that the Soviet press itself contained much data about the persecution and growth of the Underground Church. We can tell the secret now because it has been revealed.

Some Christians made a much bigger sacrifice than that of their liberties and their lives, as martyrs do. They sacrificed for Christ their integrity. They became members of the Communist Party. They tried to arrive at top positions in order to help the Underground Church.

Some of them became editors of anti-religious magazines and newspapers. Pretending to oppose the Bible, they published whole chapters of it, followed by a few words of criticism. In this way the Underground Church had pages of the Bible printed by the Communists. For the same reason, they published facts about the persecution.

Hmara was a Ukrainian. His father was a well-to-do farmer; for this 'crime' he was deported with his whole family to Siberia. Hmara grew up there with bitterness in his heart and became an anti-social element, a robber. He was put in jail for criminal offences. In jail he met Christians, who suffered with shining faces for a Lord about whom they and their lives spoke so beautifully. Overwhelmed by what he saw in them, Hmara told one of them how he had become a robber, and finished with the words, 'I am a lost man.' The Christian, smiling, asked him, 'What is the worth of a ten rouble bill when it has been lost by its owner? Is it not still worth ten roubles? Does a diamond ring diminish its value if someone has lost it? So a lost man has the whole value of a man, of a splendid creature of God. God values men even if they are sinners. And he gave his Son for them.' The old story about Jesus followed, told in simplicity with its old effect. Hmara was converted.

In 1964, he finished his term, and was released. He was no longer the old drunkard who beat his wife and children. They saw in him a new man. They, his brothers and his neighbours were converted. Hmara became a member of the Underground Church.

Later he was arrested. The Secret Police had no special motive in arresting him rather than anybody else. He was to be the subject of a new experiment.

The Communists had hands on a leading personality of the Underground Church, whom we will call Brother X. He had resisted all tortures and refused to betray. The Secret Police thought, 'What about torturing one of his flock in his presence, telling him that this torture of somebody else, of a beloved brother, would stop only if he disclosed the secrets? Worth trying.'

So Hmara was flogged, submitted to all kinds of tortures. He had the lower part of his belly split, his tongue was cut, in order to make a leading pastor become a traitor. This pastor did not betray. And what if Hmara should die? Should a pastor tremble because one of his flock will have his body killed and fall into the hand of the One who made the lilies. Hmara will have the same God on the other side of death.

Brother X told afterwards that, while Hmara was tortured, he did not think so much about Hmara. He knew that he was walking a thorny path towards heaven. But he was appalled by the sight of the sadistic joy on the faces of the torturers. He remembered that for these, too, Christ has died. And he prayed for them.

The experiment did not succeed. The corpse was returned to the family in order to scare others away from becoming Christians. But its sight produced such an indignation in the population, that the authorities could not prevent the burial from becoming a triumphal march of the Underground Church. Singing Christian songs, masses of Christians and non-Christians took the coffin to the cemetery.

As Communists usually do, they got rid of the hangmen. Those who had tortured, having been ordered to do so, were sentenced. The judge was a woman. Hearing of the ordeals, she wept. She embraced the children of Hmara. She was converted. I, who come from a Communist country, know that the sentenced hangmen were soon released, and sent to do the same things in another place.

Jesus has been given again to be crucified in the person of Hmara of Kulunda. Two brothers of Hmara are still in jail.

How do Underground Christians think? Aida Skripnikova, the heroine of the Christian youth in the Soviet Union, at the age of twenty-seven, and in prison for the fourth time (her father was shot by the Communists for his faith), writes, 'I cannot divide my heart in two, for it all belongs to the Church.' (A western Christian would have said, 'It belongs to Christ.' In the Soviet camp the Church is very much beloved. She has been seen in her splendour. There the words of old have remained true, 'Whosoever has God as his father, has the Church as his mother.' Western Christians speak about the Church rather as about a mother-in-law.) Skripnikova continues, 'Religion is my very heart and to take away my religion would be to tear out my heart.'

I met an Underground Orthodox priest from Russia. I asked him by whom he had been ordained. He answered, 'We were ten young men decided on entering the ministry. No regular Orthodox bishop would have ordained us, because they can do this only with the approval of the Communist authorities, who put unacceptable conditions. So we went to the tomb of a martyred bishop, and formed a circle round it, holding each other's hand. Two of us held the hands on the tombstone. We gave an oath of faithfulness, which we had found in an ancient book of Church history: "I take on myself scourgings, imprisonment, tortures, reproaches, crosses, blows, tribulations and all temptations of the world, which our Lord and Intercessor and the Universal and Apostolic holy Church took upon themselves and lovingly accepted. So even do I, an unworthy servant of Jesus Christ, with great love and ready will, take upon myself all these until the hour of my death." Then we prayed that Jesus might ordain us with His pierced hands. We believe He did.'

In my eyes, this ordination was valid.

Two women kneel on the steps of a warehouse in Russia. When asked why, one of them answers, 'It is a former church. It is still sacred ground. When I kneel on the steps, I can hear the priest singing the praise of God in a loud voice. You'll say that here textiles are sold and that there is no priest. I don't believe you. I believe what I hear. I smell the incense. I see the images. The worship continues. Therefore I come every night.'

Typical Russian mysticism, you will say. But why do you feel compelled to say something? Is it not better to refrain from any comment? You are on sacred ground. Who can define what is possible and impossible on holy ground?

I am Romanian, not Russian. My former Lutheran church in Bucharest is now a studio for making movie-pictures. When I walked into the building after its desecration, there could be no shadow of doubt. The angels had not left it.

When the Cathedral St. Sophia was invaded by the troops of Mohammed the Second, the priest interrupted the Liturgy and disappeared behind a door, which has remained closed since then. The Christians then believed that when Constantinople becomes Christian again, this same priest will reappear and continue the Liturgy from the very place where he interrupted it. In the 15th century, the Christians were such children. There are still children who believe that this building which has been changed first into a mosque and then into a museum, will be a church again and that the priest mentioned will serve in it. The childlike minds who believe legends have become few. My mind is among these few.

In Russia there are Christians who wear iron chains under their shirts, day and night, so as never to forget their brethren who are in bonds.

I have brought you on to most holy ground. You have shared with me scenes from the Underground Church oppressed by the Communists.

Poor Communists. They do not know the words of Tertullian, 'To kill us means to multiply us. The blood of martyrs is the seed for new Christians.' (What about sowing this seed also in the West, by sharing in the Spirit the sufferings of martyrs?) Neither do the Communists know the words of St. Hilarius, 'The Church triumphs when it is oppressed and progresses when it is despised.'

CHAPTER 2

Does the Underground Church Exist?

When, by publishing *Tortured for Christ*, *The Soviet Saints*, *In God's Underground* and other books and articles, I made known this wonderful world of Christian martyrdom and heroism, when I told this Church's story which, though real, sounds more fictitious than any novel, the response was huge. I gave up counting the letters of enthusiastic support, after they passed the figure of 300,000.

Christians simply know that they have now been told a truth which had been hidden from them. The human heart knows many things for which it does not need any proof. They knew Communism to be atheistic. They knew it to be a dictatorship.

And in the free world, as well, Christians have around them atheists, or men who are practically godless, though they might profess some form of religion. Christians know from their own experience how tyrannical a boss, a husband or a parent can be if he does not fear the Creator. They know the resistance to the terrible pressure of the world in their own hearts. When they read about the fighters of the Underground

Church who chose to die rather than compromise with the Red Dragon, they saw in their beautiful examples only a magnification under exceptional circumstances of what was best in themselves.

I received letters from some who had passed through prisons or who had worked with me in the Underground Church. A former prisoner wrote: 'What you say is as true as the fact that two and two make four.' A Romanian Lutheran pastor wrote: 'We are whole-heartedly behind you.'

But I had interesting letters from people who had quite different backgrounds. One of these came from among the Sikkim, in India, and encouraged us: 'Warmed through your most timely message, I cannot help shedding tears for all you dears. I hope that the message of the Underground Church will prepare God's children of the free world also to face such hardships in the coming day.'

I quote from a letter from Sweden: 'I heard you in a church in Stockholm. For many days afterwards, I could think or speak of nothing else than the Underground Church.'

A pastor from Bombay states: 'My colleagues have already been excited by the publications of your missions and many are telling about them to their own congregations. The demon of acquiescence to the torture of the brethren has suffered a defeat.'

An American writes: 'Please continue. The common people hear you gladly. Even if you just stir up some of us common people to prayer, you will have a very faithful ministry. Please, give our love to our brothers and sisters in the Communist countries.'

Another voice from Scandinavia: 'Do not give up. It is true that most of us sleep, but there are also those who suffer because of this laziness. There are 10,000 people

26

in our parish. At the most twenty-five come to our large church building on Sunday . . . Sometimes, a hymn is being played, without a single person opening his mouth to sing . . . I received the message of the Underground Church. It gave me a period of searching of my heart, good for me. I will read again everything which I receive from your mission and lend it to others, as often as I can. The ignorance about the Church in the East seems to be great in our country.'

Another letter from India: 'The night after reading about the martyrs I could not sleep. I pray that many people may have such sleepless nights and be aroused to prayer.' In the same spirit is a letter from France: 'The example of the Underground fighters whips us in a welcome manner. In it there is grace for all.'

And now a Briton: 'I was not a Christian. I have never been a member of any Church and I have never lived a Christian life. But I read now about today's martyrs and cannot stop weeping. Now I understand the verse,

> When I survey the wondrous cross,
> On which the Prince of Glory died,
> My richest gain I count but loss
> And pour contempt on all my pride.'

Innumerable writers show their thankfulness at having been made able for the first time to fulfil the Biblical commandment, 'Weep with those who weep.' Christians have received one of the finest gifts of the Holy Spirit, that of shedding tears for their suffering brethren.

A New Zealander: 'The things which you describe may well be repeated in our land. I have faced this possibility and decided that I am ready to suffer with Jesus, as these beloved ones have done.'

The opinion of an Englishman is, 'The type of Christianity practised in the Red Camp is much needed in our country.'

An Indian writes: 'The only conclusion I am able to draw from the message of the Underground Church is: I wish I had suffered more for Christ.' A letter from Nigeria: 'You asked me about the best way to combat the Communist threat in my country. You have supplied already the best weapon: the examples of the heroes of the martyr church.'

One letter from Ulster: 'My congregation is very earthly. My sister and I have always felt contempt towards its cold services and the stale sermons which are quite often preached. The singing in our church is so dead and heartless, that it must be an insult to our Lord. But having read about Christians going to prison for singing Christian songs and continuing to sing like nightingales, even when they are in dungeons, I am determined with Christ's strength and guidance to change this condition of things, so that the western Church may be as soul-winning as the Underground Church in countries behind the Iron Curtain.'

A Californian boy of fifteen writes that he challenged the kids in the junior high school group to give up their candy bars and malts and send money to get Bibles into Russia.

Top leaders of the churches of the free world received our message with love and opened to us their cathedrals to bring there the cry of those tortured for Christ.

But we met also some sceptics. These sceptics had not read a letter which I received by hidden channels from an officer of the Russian Secret Police: 'I read all your books and am happy that these things were told. I know that some doubt your assertions. I would recommend to these people to come and sit in a Soviet prison ten years under my command. Then they would know the truth. The only thing in your book wherewith I do not agree is that you are so mild. I, in your place, would have thundered.'

I am in the office of an important personality of the World Council of Churches.

'Your books and lectures have produced a big sensation. I take it for granted that you sincerely believe what you say, but objectively your assertions are untrue. There is no Underground Church. I have visited innumerable times Russia, Romania, and other Communist countries. I never saw the slightest trace of an Underground Church.'

I asked, 'Have you been also in China and Korea?' 'No. My travels did not take me so far. But let us stop at Russia and Romania.'

I refused. 'No, I will not stop here. Supposing that my assertions are wrong and there is no Underground Church in the Soviet Union and the European satellite countries, you have won no point. Every fourth man is a Chinese. In China, for sure, not one single church is open. One million catholics, it is reported, have been killed and a proportionate number of Protestants. The jails are full. Christians there practise their religion only underground, under the danger of torture and the death penalty. The same holds good for North Korea, Mongolia. *Nendor*, organ of the Albanian Communist Party, announced officially in November 1968 the closure of all churches. Here you have four countries about which nobody can argue. The Church there can only be underground. It suffers. Instead of debating about Russia, why not organise better help for the Chinese martyr Church?'

He was a ruddy-cheeked man, but now his face reddened even more. He said decidedly, 'Let us remain at the European countries.' I knew that I had to yield.

Otherwise the discussion would have ceased. He was a bishop and I was not. He had to remain in the right.

'Naïve people are easily impressed. And you have a gift. But I am no fool. I looked around well when I was in Russia. There is no Underground Church.' I replied, 'I have been five years in the West and have also looked around attentively. I never saw a Soviet spy. Would you say that it would be right for me to assert that there exist no such spy-rings? People who do an underground work never introduce themselves as such.'

Now he walked round the room agitated. His new shoes squeaked. I remembered how in prison I had shared one pair of shoes with a former general. Each of us went to the exercises in the yard every second day.

The bishop said ' "*Comparaison n'est pas raison.*" (Comparison is no argument.) Underground Church is an expression with a very precise meaning. We don't live in the times of the catacombs any more. An Underground Church would have to have secret seminaries, secret printing-presses, secret services, Sunday schools and so on. Such things don't go unnoticed.'

I had come to him well prepared. I took out from my bag *Nauka i Religia* (Science and Religion), the ominous atheistic magazine of the Soviet Union, dated May 1966. In it an article called '*Podpole*' (Underground) describes how a Christian with the name of Elisha created a secret seminary for young believers. It is deep in the endless Siberian woods, many miles from any house, and at a distance from the last village to which you could pass only through mire and jungle. There was the seminary—two houses. One for men and one for women. The Christians called this seminary The Academy in the Forest. The atheistic magazine mocks the secretary of the organisation of Communist youth of that district who had not the slightest idea of the existence of the seminary. But even the Christians knew about it only if they had something directly to do with the school. The rules of conspiracy were kept perfectly.

'So we have the first sign of a regular Underground Church: secret seminaries.'

I took out a book proving the existence of underground printing-presses written by the Soviet author P. Savkin and entitled *A Meeting in Hiding-Places*. It finishes by describing the arrest of Christians who have organised such a press.

I then produced a Russian New Testament printed secretly within the Soviet Union. So it is much more than a secret printing-press. They have a secret Bible Society.

My brother, who was my opponent said, 'What you say seems factual, but is not so when you take a closer look. We know about a small Baptist splinter group which did such things. Now this group has reunited with the official Church. It was a small, transitory thing. You have greatly exaggerated its importance.'

I replied, 'I am sorry to contradict you. The documents show clearly that The Academy in the Forest is Orthodox. Those arrested because of the printing-press mentioned in Savkin's book, are the Orthodox priest Pletkov and several Orthodox ladies. *Anglican Digest*, one of the organs of the Episcopalian Church of the U.S.A., says that the Orthodox Underground Church of the Soviet Union has—brace yourself—forty-five million members. The Episcopalian Church of America collaborates in the World Council with the official churches of Russia. It would have no interest in exaggerating the role of the Underground Church.

'*Headway* of January 1968, a magazine not noted for special sympathy with sectarians, says that the number of underground Baptists is four millions. If you add the

Catholics, the Pentacostals and other groups, it appears that every fourth citizen of the Soviet Union has some ties with Underground Churches. It is not a question of a small Baptist splinter group.'

I took out of my bag a pile of articles from the Soviet press and wished to show reports about secret meetings, secret Sunday schools for children. But he did not seem likely to melt like an icicle in the sunshine before my proofs.

Lenin has said that if there were important interests involved in denying that two and two make four, people would deny it. I remembered the hundreds of thousands of letters of support. People write that after having listened to the cry of the martyred Church they wept, they had sleepless nights. Others wish to be comfortable. They wish to sleep.

The bishop shook my hand. He told me, 'I sympathise with you. I understand you have suffered much. This makes you emotional. We are used to thinking factually. A man who has passed through pains like yours cannot be objective any more. Facts do not count with you. It is all sentiment.'

The door had opened already. The secretary announced the next visitor. When I closed the door behind me, it creaked. My last thought as I left him was, 'They should have an oil-can and drop a little oil into the hinges.' What thoughts pass sometimes through a human mind!

CHAPTER 3

Facts, Only Documented Facts

The episodes of the life of the Underground Church may be beautiful and impressive. But we have to distinguish between beautiful legends and impressive reality. I leave all my emotions on one side for a time and will give only facts as proven from unchallengeable sources. I cannot be quiet about them, not because of the accidents of my own destiny, which brought me into conflict with Communism, but because I love Jesus. It is written, Matthew 24:31, that His angels shall gather His elect from the four winds. If the Gospel will not be published in the Communist world, angels will find elect ones only in three winds and the word of the Master will not be fulfilled.

The Church in the Red Camp is persecuted. She needs our help. Therefore the facts of her martyrdom must be known. Even in seminaries you are taught about all kinds of churches, but never about the Underground Church, a Church existing in one third of the world. This anomaly must cease. Its existence, its suffering, its victory must be proclaimed.

The Soviet newspaper *Bakinskii Rabotchii* of the

12th of August 1971 reports the sentencing to five years of prison and to confiscation of all property of the pastor M. Grigorev. A trial against A. Filliaieva will follow. Their crime? Together with others, they have constituted 'the illegal Baptist sect' which 'strove actively' to win new members in the districts of Kirova-bad, Kasum-Ismail and Hanlarsk. The main emphasis was put upon winning youth and children of school age. Before the court, the thirteen-year-old child Anna Ivanovna witnessed unafraid and told that she worships God. The newspaper gives a long list of other children who worship together with her.

Pravda of the 19th of August 1969 describes a Baptist Underground Church in the town of Mozdok. Believers meet in an apartment with two bedrooms which are full.

The newspaper says, 'During the service people weep.' This is one of the distinguishing features of the Underground Church. I don't remember ever seeing a religious service there without tears being shed. They don't *enjoy* their sermons, they *suffer* them. They share the sufferings of Christ, the sufferings of all who suffer. They weep for those in the West who have lost the precious gift of having a tender heart and the ability to weep with those who are persecuted.

Pravda (don't forget, please, that this word means in Russia 'The Truth') describes the secret baptism of three believers. The Christians went to baptism through dark streets, avoiding men. Now, why should they be fools to be baptised secretly if the Soviet Union has religious liberty, as we are told again and again?

The same article in *Pravda* calls the fact that Christians teach love towards enemies 'treason'. The article concludes by reporting the arrest of several Christians, among them a certain Cherviakov charged with having arranged a sort of Bible Summer School for children. Twelve boys and girls have been taught there the word of God. For this crime, Cherviakov works now in bitter winter in northern Siberia's slave labour camps, knee deep in snow.

In the French Christian magazine *Tant qu'il Fait Jour* of November 1969, a Danish Christian describes his participation at an Underground Church meeting somewhere in the Soviet Union. He had the address of one of its members. Having succeeded in escaping from his hotel one evening, without attracting attention, he met in the comparative obscurity of the outskirts of the town a young girl who asked him in bad German if she could help him. He said the convened password. She asked him to follow her, going before him at a distance of some ten yards and pretending not to know him. She took him to a house where there were young people between the ages of eighteen and twenty-five. These did not need to take narcotics for kicks. To follow Jesus on the way of the cross, to worship Him under danger of arrest and death, was thrill enough. Not to attract attention, one single candle illuminated the room. At the beginning nobody spoke. After a long time of silent prayer there followed a whispered Biblical lecture. Then, one after the other, at irregular intervals, the Christians disappeared into the night. But the night was not dark for them. They were the light of dark Russia.

Zaria Vostoka, a Caucasian Communist newspaper of March 1969, reports the arrest of Peter Restshuk and others for having organised a secret printing-press in Suhum.

I can describe such a printing-press, which I have seen myself. Imagine a small state grocery. Trucks discharging goods or taking back those which had remained unsold. Nobody would notice if bales of paper were unloaded or printed material put in boxes were taken out. In the cellar of the house was a well. It was on the outskirts of a primitive town. You don't find running water everywhere in the Communist Camp. A man was let down into the deep well by a rope. From the side wall of the well, above the level of the water, a tunnel led to a small room in which was the printing-press. Those who worked there had little air. Again and again they had to leave to take a breather. Such printing-presses are discovered. Others take their place. But *The Herald of Salvation* has appeared regularly for many years. It is the underground magazine of the Soviet Baptists.

It is not only the Baptists. The Soviet Union is mainly an Orthodox country. *Sovietskaia Kirghizia* of the 15th of November 1969 tells of the Orthodox monk Zosima who had been in prison already once for his faith. After having been released, he organised a church in his parlour and held its liturgies there. The church is the house of the Christian. So it was in New Testament times. It would be much more effective in the West, too, rather than the huge buildings which exist and that are sometimes empty as regards men and often empty of Spirit.

The Communists report about this monk that Christians spoke about him in the following terms, 'The glory shines upon him,' 'God has given him a gift of speech like that of the Apostles,' 'He leads a righteous and blameless life.'

The article uses the very expression 'Underground Church' and it is the most adequate. I looked up in *Webster's Dictionary of the English Language* what the word 'underground' means, and found it to be a synonym of 'secret'. The church of monk Zosima was surely secret. Whoever wished to visit it had to have the recommendation of a trusted person and give the promise of silence, just as in the Academy in the Forest. Then you could enter the church from one street, the exit being in another. (The existence of such a church with two exits has saved my life in Nazi times.) Monk Zosima told the Christians to be as clever as serpents and righteous as doves, and, if asked, not to tell where they had been, but to invent some story.

I myself believe that St. Dominic was not mistaken when he wrote about a saintly hypocrisy. This does not mean that the end justifies the means. Just the contrary, the end to keep personal integrity and purity of heart does in no case justify the ugly means used for this purpose, which are to leave the world terrorised by the Communists without the gospel, which cannot be brought to them without using conspiratorial techniques. Moralists would call this hypocrisy, forgetting that it is immoral to leave the victims of tyrannies without the knowledge of Christ.

Zosima had also an underground workshop for the producing of candles. *Sovietskaia Kirghizia* says that many bought his secretly produced candles, which shows that there are places where there are no other possibilities of getting candles, considered as necessary for the religious services of our Orthodox brethren. The newspaper does not say what happened further to monk Zosima. But hundreds of other articles from the Soviet press justify the supposition that he must be in prison again.

More than all this. In the huge Soviet Union there exists a whole district populated only by Christians, a district about which Westerners know nothing. The world first heard about it from the Communist source *Nauka i Religia,* issue of September 1968. It tells us about large numbers of old-ritual Orthodox who took refuge in an inaccessible district in the far north of Siberia. These Christians deny the whole Soviet reality, as centuries ago Protestants denied the then oppressive Catholic reality and fled to America. *Nauka i Religia* says: 'They are a mysterious, unbelievable, newly invented world. The women and men do not recognise the anti-Christian power, but they wish a righteous death as a step towards eternal life.'

The atheistic magazine also gives several pictures taken in Siberia. Among others, it shows a copy of their Holy Scriptures. It has a great hole in the middle which has been caused by rats. They had nothing wherewith to replace it.

The Academy of Social Sciences of the Soviet Union has published a book called *Concrete Researches Of Current Religious Beliefs* (Publishing House 'MISL', Moscow).

In this book we read about many Christian groups which are all underground. All have their martyrs, though the news about them never reaches the free world. These are the Molokans, Duhobortsi, Tresvenniki, Mennonites, and others. The Communists acknowledge that 80 per cent of the Mennonite young people cling to Christ. According to this book, 'the great mass of the population of the village of Fioletovo in Soviet Armenia is composed of Molokan Christians.' Whole villages are Christian!

The atheist writers say that on Sunday mornings, as early as eight o' clock, you can see these Christians going in small groups to their illegal prayer houses. At their religious services 'there is a great percentage of young men.' The book tells us that the preachers warn them to be prepared for the second coming of Christ, because He will come unexpectedly, as a thief in the night. God looks at the life of every believer 'and He notes like the brigadier of the Kolhoz (the collective farm) in His book the good and evil done by everyone.' The preacher said openly to the Communist academician, 'I am an unhewn stone which does not fit into the foundation of Communism.'

The book acknowledges with sadness, 'In Fioletovo the Party and Communist youth organisations are small in number of members, and weak.

'In the official Baptist church of the Kazakh Republic 43% of the believers are under 50 years of age. The percentage of youth is even greater in the unregistered (underground) congregations.'

Then they describe the evenings in Christian homes with the whole family gathered around the Bible, reading it and praying.

The Communist authors tell us about the Tchurikovian Christians who are named after the founder of their group, as some Christians in the West are called Lutherans or Wesleyans, after the name of a man. These Christians read the Gospel and the book of Tchurikov, and at least twice a week they pray and fast day and night without taking any food.

According to this book there are four underground groups of Tchurikovian Christians in Leningrad alone (there might be more which have not been discovered). But there is only one official Protestant church in this town. This shows us that at least as far as the number of congregations is concerned there are many more of these Underground Churches than there are official ones.

One of the Underground Christians told the Communist researcher who questioned him, 'I have been a member of this Church for two years ... I was a believer also before this. I believed that I had to get drunk and cheat. I became conscious that this was wrong through the words of dear brother Tchurikov, and I awoke to an honest life ... I moved to Viritsa, where we have many brethren and sisters.' This group practises faith healing though it is forbidden by Soviet law and is punishable by imprisonment.

Another Underground Christian says, 'Sometimes as many as a hundred gather in somebody's house.' The book tells that 'they come together usually twice a week ... The place of the gathering always changes and is kept secret from non-members. In the village of Mihailovka we saw some such meetings in the woods, in barns and in the attics of some small houses. They protect their meetings by giving them the form of some family feast, saying that it is a birthday party or something. The love-meal (as with the first Christians) is a necessary part of their service.'

But all these are Protestant groups. The main bulk of believers in the Soviet Union belong to the Orthodox Underground. These are organised in four principal groups: 'The True Orthodox Church', 'The True Orthodox Christians', 'The Hlisti', and 'The Silent'. Suffering nuns, as those described in the book quoted above, belong to 'The Silent'. All these groups are decidedly anti-Communist and they refuse any contact with the Soviet society and with the official priests controlled by the Communist Party. The Silent even refuse discussions with Communists to protect their hearts from the poison of the godless world. They proclaim the Gospel to the Communists but don't enter into any debate. About the Hlisti the book says that there was a whole street in a village that was inhabited by them.

Anglican Digest of January 1967 estimates the number of the Orthodox Underground believers to be around forty-five million. Many are jailed every year.

I myself am not an idolatrous worshipper of facts. Every man sees what he calls 'the facts' according to a pre-existing image which hovers in his mind. It is not possible to establish facts, apart from the variety of opinions which arise when they are viewed from different standpoints. But my opponents wished facts. Here they have them.

CHAPTER 4

Russia's Golgotha

Figures show that more Christians have been suffering persecution during the Communist period than at any time in history. In the Red Camp, those who have the longest road of Calvary behind them are the children of God in the Soviet Union.

The test of the veracity of any report about the state of religion in that country is if the martyrs of today are mentioned.

When Eban, minister of external affairs of Israel, came to Western Germany, his first visit was to Dachau, the place where his co-nationals and co-religionists had been exterminated. Should Christians not learn from Jews how to behave?

I know not of one single case of a Christian church leader who, visiting Russia or any other Communist country, would have gone to place a wreath of flowers on the tomb of a martyr or who has even asked to visit the Christians in jail. Yet *Bratskii Vestnik*, the organ of the official Baptist Union of U.S.S.R., declares that a delegation of Swedish Baptist preachers visited the mausoleum of Lenin, the murderer of millions of Christians, instead of going to the grave of one of his victims. In Germany, Eban would not have gone to honour the tomb of some Nazi war-criminal. Is not the Christian religion meant to teach a higher level of solidarity with the innocent victims than the Mosaic religion?

As for us, our hearts go out to the martyrs. Not that we pity them. Their chains are of pure gold. Their cross is perfumed. All those whose spiritual senses are alive know it. To Christians, prison has always been a delectable orchard where the sweetest nectar flows. Neither do we give to the sufferings of the martyrs an honour due only to the cross of Christ. Only to this cross apply the words of St. John Chrysostom, 'The cross is the will of the Father, the honour of the Son, the joy of the Spirit, the jewel of angels, the assurance of the faithful, the glory of Paul. By the cross we know the gravity of sin and the greatness of God's love towards men.' But the true knowledge of the state of Russia's Christianity will enlarge our minds and hearts and will help us to follow in the footsteps of Christ.

Russia! Its writer Tiutchev said, 'You cannot comprehend her with your mind, you cannot measure it with any rod. She is an entity apart. You can only believe in Russia.' I, from my side, do. I believe that she will yet find peace at the feet of Christ.

We love Russia. Jesus descended into hell. So we descend into Russia's hell. When Brother Andrew, the author of *God's Smuggler*, made, in Norway, an appeal for Christian workers on behalf of Russia, two hundred volunteered at one meeting. The same thing happens now all over the free world. Young Christians expose themselves to prison sentences, but they protest against the persecutions in Moscow itself, in public squares and shopping centres. There are now innumerable Christians of the free world who can apply to themselves the words of a Russian underground poet, whose verses circulate in handwriting:

> I bend to the head of thy bed;
> You, Russia, wash
> your tears and pus
> with my blood.

The Russian martyrs are no longer alone in their fight.

There are now millions in free countries who weep with those who weep in the Soviet Union because of the closing of their beloved houses of God.

Pravda of the 18th of April 1968 says that in the district of Vologodsk there are now only seventeen churches, where there existed eight hundred before the Communist take-over. Is this because people have ceased to believe? The answer is given in the same article, 'The leaders of sects could increase their influence. Religion is not harmless in our days. It does not breathe its last as some believe, but somehow it has the tendency to go on, to attack.'

It is not her fault if she has to attack from the underground, into which she has been driven because of the closure of churches in a time when she is increasing her influence. On the 8th of April 1968 *Pravda* reports the closing of 210 churches in the Odessa region.

But how do the churches fare which have remained open? They seem to be all right in Moscow, Leningrad and a few other places visited by foreign tourists. But how about the smaller towns and villages?

A secret communication of the Underground Church tells us that on the 10th of April 1969, during a Baptist religious service in Kopeisk, a group of atheists, led by a policeman, disturbed it. They put bottles of alcoholic beverages on the Communion table and photographed the people with the bottles. These pictures will be used for atheistic propaganda.

The assertion of the Underground Church is corroborated by official communications. In *Science and Religion* of November 1967, the Communists tell what happened in the licensed Baptist Church of the village Batiatitsh. The atheist lecturer Bilchenko entered the church on Sunday, pushed aside the pastor and delivered her blasphemous doctrines. Those who had come to worship had to swallow the praise of godlessness.

Foreigners and church leaders from the West are never present at church services where this kind of thing happens.

The Psalmist loved the house of God. So does every Christian. Next Sunday when you sit comfortably in your pew, remember Russia's churches changed into warehouses, museums, factories and dancing clubs. Out of 50,000 Orthodox churches before the Revolution, only 7,000 remained. Remember the churches who have to bear the mockeries.

But the temple of the Holy Spirit is the Christian himself. Against him the great fight is fought.

A letter signed by 180 young Christians, addressed to the Soviet Government and other officials, has been smuggled out of the U.S.S.R. It is dated the 13th of May 1969, and protests against the arrest of a great number of brethren. The youngest among them, E. Radoslavov, is only nineteen years of age. (The oldest Christian prisoner about whom we know is Peter Popov. He is eighty years of age, the age of St. Polycarp when he was thrown to the lions.)

When this group of Baptists were arrested, in the school No. 61, the director Malamud told the children that the Baptists were sentenced because they had

45

sacrificed to God a girl, by crucifying her. Therefore children and parents have to beware of the Baptists.

This was not the fancy of just one man. The State Publishing House of Leningrad published a book called *Children and Religion*. In it the Communists reiterate the old lie also used in times past about the Jews, that Christians teach and practise ritual murder. Allegedly, Christians, to atone for their sins, kill their own children. The Roman persecutors had invented the story centuries ago. Now it has been unburied by the Bolsheviks to frighten the children and hinder them from becoming Christians.

Many Christians are sentenced today in the Soviet Union under the accusation of ritual murder. In 1969 the Military Publishing House of Moscow issued a book by F. Dolgich and A. Kurantov, called *We must not forget*. In it, pastor M. Krivolapov of the village Neftogorsk, district of Karaganda, is said 'to have sacrificed to God as a lamb without blemish' the three-year-old boy of the Christian Oslovetz. He allegedly killed the child in the presence of its mother and of all the worshippers. None of the faithful ever tried to hinder the horrible crime. They considered that all this happened by the will of the Holy Spirit. The child is said to have been buried during the night in a forest. The young mother died of grief.

In the Moscow newspaper *Znamia Iunosti*, Baptists are accused of having killed a girl, Vania Voinslovich, by means of ... baptism! Baptism, the Communists say, leads to pneumonia. This girl fell sick. The pastor who baptised her is guilty of murder.

Such 'facts' from Soviet publications are all lies, needless to say. Have Krivolapov and others like him been executed already for an uncommitted murder or are they in a death-row awaiting execution?

Even to be an *official* Baptist leader, licensed by the murderous Communist Government, does not necessarily save a person from persecution and years in state prisons.

Sovietskaia Moldavia of the 13th of November 1969 describes the trial of such a pastor, Slobodchikov, in Chishinau. He was known in town to have denounced the underground leader Rudenko, who received ten years in jail because of him. Rudenko died as a consequence of the tortures he endured.

So Slobodchikov knew himself to be in good standing with the Communists and imagined he was exempt from danger. He therefore dared to use a microphone at a Baptist wedding and so, as the article puts it, 'he committed the darkest of possible crimes.' A few words about Christ slipped out of his lips while speaking with the children. The newspaper says that he should have taught them rather about Paul Morozov, a Soviet hero, a child of twelve, whose statue is in one of the parks of Moscow. The heroism of Morozov had consisted in the fact that he had denounced his own father for having taken some weed from the field formerly owned by him, but now the property of the collective farm. The father was sentenced to prison. The boy had been lynched by the population.

Well, Slobodchikov had committed two crimes. He had used a microphone and, instead of eulogising a lad who had put his father in jail, had said good words about Christ who had been obedient to His parents. So Slobodchikov got two years in prison. In jail he might remember his victim, Rudenko, and repent.

The world press has announced the death in prison of the Orthodox Talantov, 1971, and of Galanskov, 1972, and the arrest of Krasnov-Levitin. The charge against them was that they protested at the lack of religious liberty in Russia, the closure of churches and the stupid burning of ikons. You can surely burn an image. But the knowledgeable Orthodox believer has never bowed before it. For him the image is transparent. He looks through the image to the holiness of Jesus, to the purity of Mary, to the courage of the martyrs painted on them. Burning images, you burn together with them many superstitious conceptions connected with them. But fire cannot burn those whose pictures have been on the images. Neither can you stamp out the love towards them in the hearts of Christians. The Christian on earth is one with Christ and with the glorified saints in heaven.

The Baptist Ivan Moiseev has been killed under tortures in the summer of 1972.

The closing of churches, the jailing of Christians, the taking away of children — all this seems insufficient to Communists. An underground document tells how aged Orthodox nuns Morozova, Gherasimchuk and Korolenko had been raped at the monastery of Pochaev.

The Moscow Publishing House issued a book *Psychosis and Religion*. They say that arguments have failed to convince religious people. Christians must be considered as mentally sick and put into asylums for the insane. We now have brethren and sisters of the faith in strait-jackets and gagged. We know the place in the town Kalinin where this institution stands.

Holger Jensen of Associated Press reported from Moscow on the 16th of May 1970 how in asylums where many Christians are interned (it being considered a sign of madness to belong to the Lord) the Communists beat the inmates every day; they tie up these men who are completely sane and kick them in the stomach. Until now, only the Canadian Association of Psychiatrists has protested against using mental institutes for torturing Christians, Jews and political opponents.

All denominations are persecuted. The Lutheran World Federation had forgotten to inform us. We had to read in the novel *This Happens More Rarely* by the Communist M. Glinka, that the largest Lutheran church in Leningrad had been converted into a swimming pool.

Unirea of January 1969 reports about the sentencing of the Catholic priest Potochniak in Lviv to five years' hard labour.

If it were not for God, the spring of vitality in the Church of the Soviet Union would be unaccountable. It blossoms under persecution. It is the fastest growing Church in Europe.

Komsomolskaia Pravda of the 15th of August 1965 wrote: 'Though the means of insult, violence and the closing of churches have been used, we not only fail to reduce the number of believers, but it seems that their number is increasing. The clandestine religious groups continue to spread.' And in the book *Atheist Education in the U.S.S.R., 1970*, (publishing house of the Central Committee of the Communist Party) we read: 'The atheist propaganda among farmers has little success.' The book gives also the explanation why. 'The farmers have been in touch with nature for thousands of years. They enjoy its gifts!'

In the town of Gomel the official Baptist Church, whose leaders have compromised with Communism, has 100 members. The Underground Church's teenager group alone has 700 members who gather in houses and in the woods and study the Bible daily at 6 o'clock in the morning before going to work.

The Underground Church is highly organised and,

escaping the surveillance of the Communist Secret Police, has gatherings at which participate Christians from the Baltic countries, from the Ukraine, from Siberia. The Underground Churches from at least five Communist countries have regular contacts among themselves. They have their own World Council of Cross-bearers. The Underground Church is not ideal. It has its weaklings and its traitors, but its predominant characteristic is heroism.

The Underground Christians make friends among the members of the Communist Party. The Soviet Press complains that when Orthodox Christians (among them many young people) wished to make a pilgrimage to the renowned monastery Pochaevskia Lavra, the Soviet administrative officials freely put trucks at their disposal (*Pravda Ukraina*, 21 November, 1971).

Sovietskaia Russia of the 6th of January 1972 reports that in the village of Meniusha, there are thirty-six members of the Communist Party. Twenty of them have holy images in their homes. Nearly all keep religious feasts and secretly baptise their children. Communists like these can only be accomplices of the Christians.

The same article tells us that the incomes of the Churches in the Soviet Union are growing. (Those of some of the major denominations in the free world are decreasing.) As for the atheistic propaganda: 'The atheistic lecturers of the districts Soletskii and Volotovsk fret and complain that they enter the halls to deliver their speeches, but the halls are nearly empty . . .' In Valda, only 26 per cent of the religious population attend atheist lectures. In Soltz and Volta, the figure is even less. The atheist lecturer, Lebedeva, acknowledges that the majority of her colleagues are insufficiently prepared to debate with believers.

The Underground Church needs your help. The wife of the Christian prisoner Peter Rumachik has been threatened that they will take away her six children because she attends Christian services with them. She writes, 'Dear brothers and sisters. Bear me up in your prayers . . . my children also, in their own childish way, appeal to you, dear mothers and fathers, that you do not cease to pray to God and do all you can that this may not happen. Dear members of the suffering Church of Christ, let us bear our sorrow and trial together as is fitting for all true Christians. When one member suffers, all members should suffer with them.'

CHAPTER 5

*How Many Christians are Jailed in
the Soviet Union?*

The only true answer is that nobody knows.

Free Trade Union News, the organ of the American trade unions, a sound proletarian source, says in its issue of April 1968 that fifty-six concentration camps have been identified in the Soviet Union. The total number of prisoners is estimated at 1,500,000. The Swedish Radio said on the 5th of November 1970 that 'in Russia there are now three million prisoners, among whom the percentage of Christians is important.'

How many suffer for their faith in God? Try to guess the right figure yourself on the basis of the following data:

On the 8th of May 1969 *Pravda Vostoka* reports from the town of Angren the sentencing of eight Christians — Friezen, Schmidt, Walla and others. They received between two and five years for having plotted wickedly to spread diseases in the population by three means: taking holy communion from the same cup, being baptised in the same baptistery, and greeting each other with a holy kiss. (The Russian Christians have the Biblical habit of kissing each other as often as they meet, and greeting each other with the words 'The peace of God be with you', instead of the ugly and non-sensical 'Hallo' or 'Hi' used by the Christians in the West. These are Bible-believing Christians. Could someone tell me where they have found a 'Hallo' or 'Hi' in the Bible? Did St. Paul greet his brethren like this?)

Well, this is Soviet justice. To go together with others to a swimming pool does not spread diseases: to be baptised with others does. Unholy kisses are immune. Only holy kisses transmit microbes. If you kiss in a holy manner, you may suffer five years in prison.

Only a month later, on the 12th of June 1969, the same newspaper announces the arrest of another fifteen people for their religious belief. These have committed the crime of going from home to home to call people to salvation. Among these fifteen is a certain Rabinchuk together with all his five sons. Stop a little and try to understand the grief of Mrs. Rabinchuk's heart. She lost on one day all the joy of her house.

So twenty-three men sentenced for their faith in the town of Angren during a single month. Twenty-three about whom we happen to know. There may be many more. We have no reason to believe that the anti-Christian terror in Angren would be fiercer than anywhere else. The Soviet Union has 5,092 towns. If in one town twenty-three go to prison for their beliefs in one month, how many Christian prisoners are there? Who knows what happens in the villages about which we never hear anything?

It is naive to reduce the problem of Christian prisoners in Russia to a couple of hundred Baptists. The Baptist prisoners themselves number more than that.

53

The Baptist Underground Church is not centralised and has no possibility of knowing what happens in the vast Soviet Union. There exist several Baptist underground groups working independently of one another.

In December 1969, the European Baptist Union announced with great joy that 'the Initsiativniki', that is the underground Baptists of the U.S.S.R., had united with the official Church. But in the same month, on the 4th, *Red Star*, the organ of the Soviet Army, announced the sentencing of a group of Baptist soldiers. Nobody knows how many, to what terms of imprisonment, under what charges. The names are not given. So much is said about them that 'the Baptists have a fierce religion and do not pity their children. They do not kill them only because the law of the state does not permit it.' In January 1970, after the 'reunion' staged especially for foreign delegates, the whole underground activity continued, as well as its denunciation by the Soviet press.

There must be thousands of Baptists in prison. *Kristeligt Dagbladet*, Copenhagen, of the 4th of March 1970, evaluates them at 10,000.

In my book *The Soviet Saints* I have provided many instances of sentencing of Pentecostals. In my hearing before the U.S. Congress Committee, I gave names of persecuted Seventh Day Adventists. Forty Catholic priests from Lithuania signed a protest, dated August 1969, against the sentencing to forced labour of Rev. M. Gylys and Rev. J. Sdepskis. Miss Paskeviciute, a Roman Catholic who had prepared children for their first confession, was also deported to a forced labour camp, where she died of over-exhaustion. But the great bulk of Christian prisoners are the Orthodox, these constituting the majority of the Soviet population.

The official Orthodox Church has a membership of

fifty millions, according to the claim made by its delegation at the session of the World Council of Churches in New Delhi. The Orthodox underground is considered to have another forty-five millions. Then there exists the so-called True Orthodox Church and Old Ritual Orthodox. All these give huge numbers of prisoners. Sometimes we read about them in the Soviet Press. Some other news we have from underground documents. But the names of most of the martyrs are known by God alone. Then there are sufferers from all kinds of Christian sects which exist only in the Soviet Union as the Molokans, the Duhobortal, the Murashevtzi and others.

Those who know best, men who are actually in Soviet jails today, smuggled out a letter, published in *Posev* of December 1970. They write: 'As before, Russia is covered by a net of camps ... of forced labour ... Through these camps passes unceasingly a human stream of millions of men.' The letter is signed by the Christian prisoner Platonov, by the writer Ghinzburg and by several other well-known personalities, who sit in prison today.

Christians, being the main force opposed to Communism, must have a high share in this number of millions.

Again *Posev* gives us the names of a few of them detained in the camps of Mordovia (U.S.S.R). Among them is Nadezjda Groshova, charged with appertaining to the true Orthodox Church. This is the Orthodox Church which worships in the catacombs, not acknowledging the priests and bishops who have compromised with Communism. One female prisoner has been released after twelve years in jail, when she attained the age of ninety.

The Underground Church is the most powerful anti-

Communist force in the Soviet Union. It is also the most organised. If the figure of 1,150,000 political prisoners is correct, a big percentage must be the religious opponents, considered by the Communists as political criminals. The Communists themselves say again and again that religion is their No. 1 foe.

How many Christians are in prison in the Soviet Union? Nobody knows. Remember this, however: in one town twenty-three were sentenced during one single month. There are 5,092 towns and there are twelve months in a year.

Perhaps after these grim things we should smile a little, even if it will be a bitter smile.

Moscow News, the newspaper in English which appears in the capital of the Soviet Union, says in its issue of the 25th of October 1969, 'All religious associations in the country (Baptists, Mennonites, Methodists, Adventists, Molokans, Pentecostals and even Jehovists) have the right freely to observe their rites at specially allotted premises.' The newspaper did not say that the premises were prison cells.

Michel Zhidkov, one of the top leaders of the official Baptist Union of U.S.S.R., declared at the European Baptist Congress in August 1969 in Vienna that nobody is persecuted for his faith in his country. Michel Zhidkov's own father spent many years in Siberia because he had dared to believe in Christ contrary to the orders of the Communist dictators. Not one delegate booed Michel Zhidkov.

But there is a good side to the fact that many Christians are jailed in the Soviet Union.

The prisoner Basil Kozlov tells in a letter, smuggled out to us, not only about his conversion but that 'the Soviet prisoners and concentration camps are the place of spiritual re-birth and meeting with Christ for a great number of people.'

Released in 1957, after having finished his sentence for robberies, he became a member of the Underground Church. Since then he has been condemned four times to a total of ten years of prison, but this time it was for his faith. The officers of the Secret Police told him: 'It would have been better for you to remain a bandit than become a Christian.' At one of his trials, the prosecutor said: 'Look to the past of this Kozlov! He has been a thief and now he pretends to be a holy apostle,' to which Kozlov replied: 'Yes, I was a bandit and for this I have taken my punishment. But I died to sin and to the past. The power of the Blood of Jesus has cleansed my criminal heart. Now I am a new man; what the prosecutor shows are relics.'

We have many testimonies that Siberian prisons have become hotbeds of Christianity.

Risking a new sentence, Kozlov wrote from prison to Kosygin, Brezjnev, etc.: 'If you would not hinder the Christians who are in prison even today to speak about Christ to this miserable world, how much the life of thousands of sinners would be changed! You would not need to keep one million lecturers to propagate an atheistic morality. You would not need so many policemen. The money you use to lead a war against God could be better spent for publishing Bibles for our Soviet people. We would have then less drunkards and thieves and less crime. Then the prison camps could be emptied and you could change the jails from museums of human savagery and atrocity.'

The Belgian magazine *Panorama* of the 9th of May 1969 publishes that one of the former heads of the Gestapo, Henrik Mueller, sought as a war-criminal, is now leader of Moscow's Communist Secret Police.

He has tortured Christians and Jews in times past in Hitler's name. He does the same job now in the name of Karl Marx's ideals. The important thing for him is to be able to torture.

Men like him, and his genuine Communist comrades, do not feel it is wrong to commit cruelties, just as we do not feel it cruel to peel potatoes. For Marxists, man is only matter. They do not believe in the existence of soul or spirit. We cut wood, we tear down houses, we hammer nails into walls. It is matter. We have no remorse. So, Communists do not pity their victims. For them they are matter.

CHAPTER 6

The Prison Regime

We could describe the regime in Soviet prisons from communications smuggled out by the Underground Church. But these might be considered as biased. So I prefer to allow a Communist to tell the story.

Under Dubcek, there was a short respite in Czecho-slovakia. You could tell some of the truth. At that time a certain Loebl, an old-time Communist, high-ranking official of the Ministry of Foreign Trade, told the story how he has been tortured by his own comrades under Novotny, in a time when the Czech Secret Police was led by Russian specialists. Loebl's story, corroborated by writings of other Communists who have passed through the same ordeal (see Arthur London's *The Confession* and the book of Mrs. Slanski about her husband being hanged by his own comrades), will give us a picture of what our brethren have to endure in Soviet prisons and will give us the chance of fulfilling the commandment, 'Remember them that are in bonds, as bound with them' (Hebrews 13:3).

I quote from the Czech Communist magazine *Reporter* of the 15th of May 1968. Loebl writes that during the interrogations, which lasted an average of sixteen hours a day, he was not allowed to sit. He had to stand or march sixteen hours a day, day after day. All the time he was hungry. After a fortnight, his feet were swollen, every inch of his body ached at the slightest touch. Sometimes he had to stand for a whole day with his face to the wall. Even the latrines were of the stand-up type.

Loebl was drugged. So was I. So are Christian prisoners in the Soviet Union. 'All of a sudden I would feel as if someone were trying to push his hand into my head. It was a sensation similar to that which one has after laughing-gas has been administered as an anaesthetic . . . I heard from other prisoners, who had to do the cleaning at the prison hospitals, that they had found empty bottles of narcotics, which were put into the soup served to prisoners.

'In addition to classical beatings, there were ice-cold showers, the crushing of genitals; or the victim's head was wrapped in a wet cloth, and when this cloth dried and shrank it caused unbearable pain . . . I was no longer a person.'

During this short respite in Czechoslovakia we heard what is happening continually in the Soviet camp but remains untold. The Czech Communist newspaper *Kulturny Zhivot* of the 31st of May 1968 reads: 'The church as a whole has been in prison since 1950 . . . In jails, guards fired from the observation towers into the cells. Dogs without muzzles were led into the prison hospital, the inmates were beaten on their heads with horse-whips and sprayed with water from hoses. The investigators yelled, "We do not recognise any humanitarianism." Many of the inmates suffered internal injuries. Hermanovsky was a very young man, but became insane from the torture. In one of the transports was also the seventy-five-year-old bishop Vojtassak. They stripped him naked and he had to stand for several hours on the stone floor. When he could not continue the squatting exercises, they yelled at him, "Squat, until you spit blood, you . . ." '

At that time, the late professor of theology, Hromadka, Czech himself, was touring through all the continents for the World Council of Churches telling of religious liberty.

Don't read only the story of these tortures. But feel them as if you are being tortured, because in reality it is you. All Christians are one soul and one heart. They constitute the mystical body of Jesus Christ. When one member suffers, all the members suffer together with him. Never would a mouth say, 'I don't care. It's not me, it is the tooth or the stomach which aches.' It would rather say, 'I have pains,' and all the members would collaborate to evince or ease the pain.

With a hard look in his eyes, with a face which had grown grey from care, a leading personality of the German Lutheran Church warned me: 'No point in publicising such facts. It will only make things to become worse.' My hands began to quiver, and I said with vehemence, 'It was centuries ago that the Chinese might have refused to rescue a drowning man for fear of antagonising the water demons. Such a mentality is obsolete in the twentieth century. Crocodiles do not eat men because zoologists have upset them by writing about their voracity, but because it is in their character. Russian Communists began with torturing Christians when I was the age of nine. They will continue to do it, and even grow in ruthlessness, because this is their teaching, not because I protest against the terror and organise relief for those persecuted.'

CHAPTER 7

Red China

An ingenious person has estimated that if a man stood by a roadside and watched the entire population of China walk past him at the rate of one individual per second, more than twenty years would elapse before the last member of the procession went by. But in this huge and steadily increasing crowd, very few would be Christians.

Even before the Communist take-over, there was in China only one Christian to 475 non-Christians. We must be aware of the quantitative insignificance of missionary work. Ten per cent of the population of the world are English-speaking. They have ninety per cent of the preachers and pastors. Only ten per cent of the preachers work among the ninety per cent of those who have committed the sin of being non-English-speaking and belong therefore to the spiritually under-developed peoples. As far as I know, Norway and Northern Ireland are the exceptions, and the missionary effort of churches in other western countries is minimal. From the immeasurable incomes of the churches of the U.S.A. only six per cent is used for charitable and missionary purposes. We have not fulfilled the great commission, 'Go and teach all nations.'

In China, the Christians have always been a small minority.

And now the Christians had to face the onslaught of a new religion, 'the Mao worship'. Giant Mao statues began going up throughout the length and breadth of China. Millions were mesmerised by the method of brainwashing brought to its final perfection.

Many of the influential Christian leaders had not realised the danger of Communism. Some had sympathised with it. Others would confine themselves to what they understood to be a pure Gospel, not mentioning the Communist menace because this would mean becoming involved in politics. But when Communist politicians enter the sphere of religion, introducing there their poison or persecuting the children of God, politics is forced upon us. It cannot and should not be avoided. Who thinks that he can separate religion from politics, knows neither religion nor politics.

Just mark in your Bible all the parts which have political connotations. You will find they are seventy per cent of Scriptures. The formation of a nation, the freeing of slaves, minute laws regulating state life, rules of judges and kings, prophets expressing their thoughts about big empires and nations surrounding the Jews, 'Render to Caesar', 'be submissive to authority', and also the description of these authorities as wild beasts in Daniel and Revelation, all these and many other parts of the Bible are political. Christians must speak out on political questions, only without distorting politics with personal greed or national ambitions.

In any case, the Chinese Christians were unprepared for the onslaught. When the Communists took over China, Communism had ruled Russia already thirty years. Nothing was taught in Chinese churches and seminaries about the experiences and methods of work of the Underground Church. The examples of the Russian martyrs were not known.

No bells ring any more on the mainland of China under Communist occupation. All the churches have been closed and desecrated, except three or four for the staffs of embassies and foreigners.

An eye-witness who escaped to Hong Kong reports about the stoning to death of a Christian girl in a Communist slave-labour camp. She was bound hand and foot, and made to kneel in the centre of a circle of people who were commanded to stone her. Those who refused to participate were shot. The eye-witness says that she died with her face shining, like St. Stephen. One at least of those who saw her was led to faith in Christ through that girl who sealed her testimony with her blood.

Five students who were sent out to dig deep holes into which they were then placed, sang Christian hymns as they were buried alive.

A leader of our German Mission brought back from Hong Kong the news that in a southern town a group of some thirty Underground Christians was discovered. They were dragged on to the streets, veins at their throats were opened, and so they died. This was in May 1970.

Now we have the news from Kwangsi about a pastor beaten to death. We have to withhold his name so as not to endanger his family.

Vart Land of the 11th of February 1969 reports how a pastor from the district of Swatow had been dragged through the streets with a dunce's cap on his head. The cap had ugly inscriptions on it. Faithful pastors would be led, with shaved heads, in mocking processions, exposed to revilings. But these pastors continued to gather their flocks in small groups, usually not larger than four to ten people.

Christians have to kneel in the streets. They are spat upon. With some, their hair was cut, leaving them with only a cross as a mark that they are Christians.

Radio Moscow said on the 7th of April 1969 'In the course of ten years, more than twenty-five million people in China were exterminated . . . The discontented were dumped by the millions into enormous concentrations camps.'

The Moscow newspaper *Krasnaia Zvezda* of the 7th of May 1969, wrote: 'The Chinese communist party . . . have burnt people's eyes out with boiling water and sulphuric acid, hacked off limbs with penknives and split open skulls with stones and ancient broad-swords.'

All religions are persecuted alike. *Tibetan Review* of the 15th of July 1971 publishes an appeal by the Buddhists of Inner Mongolia (a province of China). In it we are told that the Communists cut out the tongue of Lama Huh-lu (a Buddhist monk), cut off all the fingers on the hands of teacher Saranchulu, and burnt alive the child of a woman named Nominerdene. The teacher Munhbish had his genitals and face burnt with branding irons. He has lost his reason. Damba, Dambii and Dambalab were hanged from a tree by their thumbs and boiling water was poured over their heads.

The most minute descriptions of the tortures inflicted upon prisoners, among whom are many Christians, have been given by their Russian comrades, upset against them for a while. A thief whom I knew in prison had very high moral principles! He told me once that he condemned decidedly, and considered as unethical any theft committed by somebody other than himself. That is how the Russian Communists think. They demand the monopoly of directing the torturing of innocents in the whole world. The Chinese Communists, not being obedient in this, are denounced now for their cruelty, learned in the Soviet Union, by *Literaturnaia Gazeta*, a Moscow magazine (quoted in *Russkaia Jizn* of the 18th of June 1969).

During one torture called 'the small criticism', the man is paraded through the street having a dunce's cap on his head, with an inscription on his breast listing the charges against him. This continues for three consecutive days. After parades, he has to fulfil the dirtiest and heaviest work. He receives food only once a day, but before receiving the food he has to bow ninety times to the earth, before the portrait of Mao.

If this treatment does not re-educate him, then follows the 'big criticism'. With hands tied behind his back, he has to attend daily meetings for two months. At these meetings his sin of not believing in Mao is exposed. He is ruthlessly beaten and spat upon. After every meeting, again the respectful ninety bows before the picture of Mao.

The third torture is called 'airplane'. A rod is put upon the man's shoulders. The hands, tied to the back are strung upwards towards this rod, until they are out of joint. In this position he has to bow 180 times before the one who is better than all gods.

During the torture called the 'Golden Scale' a heavy desk is placed on the shoulders of the guilty one. On each side of the desk the Red Guards put three bricks. With the bricks on his shoulders, he has to stand at attention before the picture of Mao for two hours. Every twenty minutes, a brick is added on each side. In the end he has eighteen bricks to bear. Woe to him if they move. If he bows his knees even a little bit, the whole torture begins again.

Another torture is to shave the heads of Christians and to put ashes on them. So they must stand at attention before the sacred ikon of Mao. No moving is allowed.

Paster Dries van Voillie was kept without any sleep for *twenty-one days and nights*. Then, chained with his hands behind his back and shackles on his feet, he had to squat and immediately get up again; then squat once more: this ceaselessly. The hands, chained behind the back, were lifted by a soldier higher and higher, a torture producing great pain. Then he was brought back into his cell, where fellow-prisoners who had yielded to Communist pressure made him continue the squatting exercises during whole nights. They all spat upon him. At a certain moment he had the hallucination that those who spat on him were his friends, pastors like himself. He could not understand what was happening to him. In the end he reached the conclusion that he must have committed horrible crimes, and acknowledged to have done spy-work—to have been in the service of an Imperialist Police Agency—to be guilty of the most terrible things. (Some Western church leaders consider such confessions as valid.) He had to prove the sincerity of his confessions by denouncing others. At moments like these, some of our brethren commit suicide.

A Christian bore all the humiliations, but refused to bow, answering again and again, 'I know one single thing: there is a God. Apart from this, I know nothing.' (He had not read the 'God-is-dead' theologians.) He answered again and again: 'Do with me whatever you like, but I will not deny my faith.' Brave Sung-Fu. We do not know his end.

Christians were obliged to hand over their Scriptures and religious books in order that they should be burned publicly. To some their own hearts told them, others had learned it from church history, that in the early centuries whoever handed a Scripture to the persecutors was expelled from the Church for ever.

Christ is the Word of the living Father. So are the Scriptures. To give the Scriptures to be burned is like giving Christ to be killed. There were Christians who realised the respect due to the written word of God. They hid the Bible. *Asian News Report* of March 1968 says: 'In Canton, a Christian lady who had hidden her Bible in a pillow was subjected by the Red Guards to the grossest humiliation. She was stripped naked, smeared all over with honey and made to stand in the fierce sun for many hours.'

Parcels from abroad, containing Bibles, are returned with a slip stating that its teaching is 'against the law and morality of the People's Republic of China.'

To possess a Bible is to be in deadly danger. A brother who had been sent there from the West to help, was taken by a Chinese Christian into his room. He closed the shutters to be sure nobody saw from the outside. Then he removed some boards from the floor. There he kept a Bible and hymnal. When he was sure he was not observed, he would take them out and read them.

The well-known book by the German Christian Rittling, entitled *Red or Dead*, states that Red Guards are burning men with red-hot pokers. There have been cases of crucifixion. But the same report states that sometimes Communists preferred to be jailed instead of continuing to be torturers of Christians. One of them was overheard saying, 'If we cut out their tongues and forbid the Christians speech, they love with their hands, with their feet and with their eyes, they love always and everywhere until their last respiration. Does nobody know how to take out the power of love from these stupid Christians? Does nobody know a way to put hands on their Christ?'

Very few pastors survived. One of them writes: 'In order to continue to live we have become farmers, mechanics, artisans . . . in these conditions we are still happy . . . We are unswervingly optimistic. If not today, tomorrow certainly this vast country will be Christianised.'

When they are caught doing their underground work, they suffer beyond description. At Tientsin, a pastor subjected to excruciating interrogation by the Communists, fearing that his resistance might fail him and then result in harm to others, literally tore out his own tongue. A normal man cannot do it; one maddened by torture can.

Mao Tse-Tung kicks against the pricks. He has a powerful leaning toward Christ. In 1936, though long since a Communist leader, when he was dangerously ill he asked to be baptised. A Franciscan Sister baptised him. We know it from Cardinal Yu-Pin. (*National Catholic Register* of the 8th of November 1970.)

The Christian Church at Midnight

A refugee in Hong Kong tells that in a little Christian
cell-group of the commune where he was made to en-
gage in forced labour, they would meet together in the
very early morning in a basement, before they went to
work. If they were not able to meet together, they would
join two by two in the early hours, as they walked to
work and, on the pretext of being engaged in conversa-
tion, they would quietly quote Scripture verses to each
other. How well it is for those who have gathered a
treasury from the word of God in their hearts!

This little cell group was discovered by the Communists. The refugee and his friend were put in prison.
His friend died there.

Chinese prisons are real hells: dirty, humid, cold and
full of insects. It is considered that some forty thousand
Protestants are today in prison. The number of Catholics must be higher.

But the dirty cells are the setting for episodes of
heavenly beauty.

Two Christians trembled from cold in a cell. Each
had a thin blanket. One of the Christians noticed how

the other trembled, and the thought shot into his mind, 'If that were Christ, would you give him your blanket?' Of course he would. He immediately spread the blanket over his brother.

Next day they were given more blankets.

The Christian prisoners have to pass through brainwashing. Communist indoctrinators visit them regularly while they are sitting in the yard of the prison.

One Christian, when the Communist tried to convert him to his beliefs, wrote on the sand the Chinese characters for righteousness. The Chinese letters are painted rather than written. The ideogram for 'righteousness' in Chinese is showing a lamb over the personal pronoun 'I'. The Christian asked the Communist 'Could you tell me what this character means?' He answered correctly, 'Righteousness'. Then the Christian pointed to the lamb over the I and quoted from the New Testament, 'Behold, the Lamb of God which takes away the sins of the world', the Lamb of God which covers the sinful 'I'. The Communist indoctrinator walked out silently. He might have had a Christian background himself.

Two Christians were led towards torture and death. 'It is finished now,' said one in a whisper. His brother answered, 'No, this is not what Jesus said when He suffered. His words were "It is accomplished."'

By His cross Jesus redeemed mankind. In order to bring souls to salvation made possible by the Redeemer, others must be ready to bear crosses. Our Chinese brothers and sisters, when they endure water being forced up their noses, pieces of wood put between the knuckles and compressed tightly, severe electric shocks and even crucifixion, share the sufferings of Jesus for the salvation of mankind.

Not only the heroes of faith suffer. China's Church had not only faithful but also treacherous leaders. No wonder. The first band of apostles had a Judas. These traitors had collaborated with the Communists from the first, leading astray the rank-and-file believers and making 278,000 sign the Communist manifesto.

Communists love treason, but not the traitor. After having used them, the Reds sent the traitors to sit in prison together with the faithful Christians whom they had denounced. They now have time for reflection in their dirty cell. What is better? Compromise with the tyrants or purity of soul?

Many pastors committed suicide out of fear of betraying secrets of the Underground Church in some moment of weakness. We know also Christian laymen who did the same.

Others went mad. For example, Rev. Beda Tsang, who was compelled to repeat continually, 'Tsang Beda, 47 years of age. Tsang Beda, 47 years of age.' He was deprived of sleep until he died.

Some told me, 'I could not bear to read your books to the end. They give me sleepless nights.' This is just what I aimed at. I wished you to find fellowship with those to whom sleep is denied. I have known a prisoner to whom sleep was denied twenty-five days and nights.

China had 6,000 missionaries before the Communist take-over. Now they have not a single one. Some missionary agencies make big plans for an uncertain future when the doors of China may reopen. No, I am for breaking down the doors. We cannot allow millions of Chinese to die without the knowledge of Christ in the hope that in a future generation others will die saved. God tore in two the veil in the temple of Jerusalem. Why not tear the Bamboo Curtain? Why not penetrate with the Gospel into Red China secretly, risking imprisonment and death? The multitude of missionaries who died in China during the Boxer rebellion and the martyrs of Communist times, now glorified saints in heaven, call us to follow their example.

CHAPTER 9

Romania: a Liberal Communist Country

I had a whole committee of church leaders before me.

'Your fault, Mr. Wurmbrand,' said one of them, 'is that you mix up things. You put all Communists in the same pot. I admit that things are very bad in Red China (that is what the Chinese Christians have, from his point of view — an admission of the tortures they endure. And what a rich church this interlocutor of mine represented!). Things could be better in Russia, too. But I have just returned from Romania. You cannot deny that full liberty exists there!'

Pleased with himself, he looked around to his colleagues. Then he stretched out his hand towards me: 'Would you contest it?' From some hands power emanates: none emanated from his.

About Romania, the opinion seems to be unanimous. The Pope, the World Council of Churches, the Bible Society, the Lutheran World Federation, the Baptist Union — what a unity of opinion. In praising the liberty of religion under the Romanian Communists even Pentecostal leaders agree with the Pope.

They all have a virtue which I don't have — candour.

A naïvety which makes them see geese as swans.

In January 1968, the Pope received the Prime Minister of Romania and the Minister of External Affairs, Mr. Manescu. At that time, some 1,200 Greek Catholic churches had been stolen. They were not given back after this visit. All the Greek Catholic bishops except one had died in prison. *Unirea* of June 1969 reports that Romanian Greek Catholic priests and laymen have received a total of five thousand years of imprisonment. All their schools and philanthropical institutions had been confiscated. The Pope shook hands with the murderers of his flock. Blessed is he if he used the opportunity of this visit to call them to Christ.

After this visit, from the five dioceses of the Roman Catholic Church, the situation continued that only one had a titular bishop. The Roman Catholic bishops had also died under torture. The one surviving, Marton Aron, is not allowed even to visit his priests.

He could not attend the Council of Bishops in Rome, but when foreigners were gathered for the anniversary of 250 years since the building of a famous monastery, he was led by force and under threat was compelled to be present.

A Western bishop who visited Romania published a report in his diocesan magazine. In his article the word 'dinner' occurs six times, the word 'luncheon' five times, and once the word 'breakfast'. (This has nothing to do with the etymology of the word. There has been no fasting. What he ate did not break a time during which he would have fasted.) Not once does the word 'martyr' appear. His fellow-bishops had been martyred. Now the Western bishop has eaten at table with their executioner, Dogaru, and he praises the dinners. They had been really good.

There appear in Romania religious and patriotic

magazines, which have only one defect: nobody sees them in Romania. They are for foreign use only. If anyone does not believe this, let him ask at a kiosk in Bucharest for *Glasul Patriei* (Voice of Fatherland). He'll not obtain it. But you can get it easily everywhere in the West and so be persuaded what good magazines appear in Romania.

In one issue Father Staniloaie praises greatly the religious liberty in Romania. He himself has been in prison for five years, together with me. He writes under compulsion.

I was interrupted. The one who did so, a short, bald man, with light eyes, told me in all sincerity, 'There have been bad things in the past. But Ceausescu has changed.'

I replied, 'And where are T. Dumitrache, Iorgu Stavar, Elena Sincai? They were arrested at Christmas 1968 having committed the crime of demonstrating on the street, demanding religious liberty. Since then they have disappeared. It is feared that they may have succumbed to the harsh prison regime.' (*Bire* of the 1st of December 1969.)

The Romanian Communists lie just like the others. They have asked American Baptists and Pentecostalists to give dollars, for which they will build churches for these denominations. But why give dollars for this? Two-thirds of the Romanian-speaking Baptists, Pentecostalists, Brethren and Adventist Churches have been closed and the buildings confiscated. Why not restore and re-open these?

The aim of Romanian Communists is the same as that of Leninists all over the world: the destruction of religion. *Romania* of the 5th of June 1969 announced that Mihai Gere, one of the Communist Party secretaries, speaking at a meeting of the National Council of

'Pioneers', the Red Children organisation, said that the political education of the pioneers was inadequate, because there was insufficient emphasis on atheistic and anti-religious orientation.

Romania a country of religious liberty? The Bible Society is forbidden. The same is true of the Y.M.C.A., the Salvation Army (called there 'Army of the Lord'), the Church of the Nazarenes, and many other organisations.

Nobody is allowed to be a Baptist, or Pentecostalist, or Adventist preacher without the licence of the Government, which is given only if the Communists are sure that you will preach as they permit. Believers' baptisms must be authorised by the Commissioner of the Government. He authorises an average of twenty-five per cent of the requested baptisms. So the practice of secret baptism exists, performed during the hours of darkness. Those who are caught are sentenced.

In January 1970 we received the news of the sentencing of the Baptist deacons — Gheorghe Potoc of the village of Leasa, Lupei Vasile of the village of Bontesti, Popa Ioan from Sic and Florea from Suseni — for the crime of having been baptised illegally.

In 1973 the pastor Moise Urs of Timishoara was sentenced to ten years in prison.

To protect others from being arrested, Christians often turn to self-baptism. They go alone to a river and submerge in the water after having said, 'I baptise myself in the Name of the Father, and of the Son and of the Holy Ghost.'

From 165 Baptist pastors the licence to preach has been withdrawn. The number of Orthodox monasteries has been reduced from 182 to 74; the number of monks and nuns from 6,097 to around 2,000. There are in

Romania 800 Greek Catholic priests who are not allowed to fulfil their vocation because they did not comply with Communist orders.

CHAPTER 10

The Absolute Torture

A government cannot be judged only according to what it does now. We must have in view also what it has experimented with, its future purpose and what it is prepared to do. The government of the Soviet Union wages no war. But it has experimented with the nuclear bomb and stockpiles it. So do other governments.

In the same way, whoever wishes to judge the religious situation in Romania must remember that members of its government, or of the Central Committee of the Party in power, now include Ceausescu, Maurer, Manescu and Bodnaras, among others.

Romania was the laboratory for experimenting in the perfect torture which breaks the power of will.

The big innovation of Russian and Chinese Communists has been the application of Pavlov's brainwashing technique to the re-education of prisoners. The results have been astonishing. Remember only what an enormous percentage of American prisoners of war in Korea became collaborators with the Communists. Remember the Bolsheviks like Zinoviev, Kamenev,

Bukharin, confessing to crimes they had not committed, and pathetically demanding that death sentences should be passed upon them. Remember Cardinal Mindzenthy confessing that he had been a spy and a black marketeer.

But Pavlov's method, the result of many experiments on dogs, is not perfect, because men are not like dogs. You can create conditioned reflexes in men, but here you will encounter also resistance to the forming of these reflexes. I myself have been subjected to brainwashing techniques for nearly three years and my brain still remained in a state which the Communists would consider dirty.

To brainwashing you can oppose heartwashing. While the brainwashing indoctrinator talks without much conviction what is commanded of him, you can repeat to yourself silently but endlessly some short proposition, always the same, in the contrary direction. When the brainwashers said, 'Christianity is dead', I repeated to myself again and again, 'Christ is alive.'

But Romania has been the place of tortures which can break any power of resistance.

Christians could bear beatings on genitals, being strung to ropes, standing on tiptoes for hours, the tying of hands and feet behind the back and hoisting the victim into the air, the slamming of fingers in a door, etc., when these things were done by the Communist foe.

The Romanian Communists invented the torturing of Christians and patriots *by their fellow-prisoners*. A Communist officer would finish torturing after a couple of hours. With the fellow-prisoners you were in the same cell day and night. This torture never ended. Secondly, from a Communist you did not expect anything else than ordeals. But it was terrible to see a fellow-Christian, with whom you had taken Communion earlier, or with whom you had worked in a patriotic organisation, finding now delight in torturing you in a most refined manner. He has been corrupted and forced to do this by promises that he will be released, by threats, or by having himself first passed through torments in which he proved weak. The refinement of cruelty consisted in the fact that the Christians corrupted by the Reds would first pray with you who were completely unaware that they had become Communist tools, or they would speak about the Gospel and at a certain signal jump at you to inflict terrible ordeals.

When I came out from Romania, I had reservations. I did not say everything that happened in Romanian prisons. I had not witnesses to prove my assertions, which would have seemed unbelievable. Therefore I did not describe all the suffering and nightmares. Now I have the testimonies.

Mr. D. Bacu and Ion Cirja, former fellow-prisoners, have published books about the perfect torture by the Communists in our country. Unfortunately, these books are available only in Romanian.

I quote from the book of Mr. Bacu, called *Piteshti*, which is the name of a Romanian town, with a famous prison. The very name of the town comes from the Slavic word *pitka*, which means 'torture'. What predestination there is in names sometimes! The things which he describes have happened just the same also in other jails. Remember these tortures were practised not by Communists (though under Communist guidance), but Christians tortured Christians, patriots tortured patriots.

'We had to scrub the floors while two or three other prisoners rode on us . . . We were obliged to eat like the swine. We had to kneel, with the hands hand-cuffed to the back, lapping the hot soup from the dish. At noon, bread was thrown before you, which you had to eat in the same position, using only the mouth. The last crumb had to be gathered from the floor with the lips or tongue. The whole day you had to sit at the bedside with the feet stretched out, with your hands on the knees, head up, looking straight forward without the right to move. After sixteen hours of such torture, you were allowed to sleep, but only on your back, the face upwards, the body per-fectly stretched, with the hands over the blanket. If you changed your position you were hit powerfully with a stick by the one who watched.

Sixteen prisoners were put one over another. Un-der the pressure of this weight, the muscles of the abdomen of the last yielded. He made in the cell what he was not allowed to do in the toilet. He was compelled to cleanse his undertrousers with his tongue. He refused first. His fingers were bruised between two pieces of wood. In the end . . . The student A.O. was compelled to fulfil his necessities in his dish, then to receive the food in the same dish and to eat. The student N.V., not successful in cutting his veins, put his head in the bucket of hot food, hoping to die. He did not die. (Christians trying to commit suicide! What a nice subject of moral indig-nation in the free world, from the side of those who eat apple pies!' Some tried to tear out their veins with their teeth.

It was forbidden to hit upon the temples, in the re-gion of the heart, in the neck, wherever death might follow. They did not wish physical death . . . They made a devilish experiment: the death of the soul, putting in its place conditioned reflexes. Not physical, but moral death.

At Easter, they clothed a prisoner in sheets, he having to play the role of Jesus Christ. Out of soap they made a genital organ, which the theological student, the would-be Christ, had to wear on his chest instead of the cross. He had to walk around the room, beaten with sticks—the road to Golgotha. Other Christians had to bow before him, to kiss this genital organ and say, "I bow before your Almightiness." There was only one who would not accept to descend to such blasphemy. He was tortured for hours.'

I have told in my book *God's Underground* what happened to an Armenian Catholic priest who was compelled to say the Holy Mass over excrements and urine. I did not venture to say everything then. Now that it has been said by others, I can add: those who compelled him to do this were corrupted fellow-Christians who previously had confessed to him, prayed with him, who had been instructed to play their role perfectly. When he relied on them as being his flock, they tortured him until he became half-mad and did whatever he was commanded. May I add, that after being released from prison, he confessed his sin to another priest. This was reported to the hierarchy and as a result he was excommunicated. I consider that the church leaders of the West who did not move a finger to help us should have been excommunicated instead.

I have known an Adventist farmer whose toes were cut off by his former fellow-Christians, slowly, at intervals. The cutting was done bit by bit and lasted for weeks.

Later on, some of these corrupted Christians had

terrible excesses of remorse. My former fellow-prisoner, Ion Carja, tells the story of one who plunged his head, down to the shoulders, in a big bucket of faeces and urine. With the dregs on his face, he cried, 'Don't wash me. So I wish to remain. What I have on my face is nothing. My soul is dirtier.' He had tortured to death his brethren in the faith. I will not tell you how far I went to transpose myself into the situation of this poor, precious soul, beloved by Christ, who had gone astray. But I could identify myself with him, feel his dirt as mine, his guilt as mine, and be sure that I was not a little bit better than he. That is what Christ did when He took our guilt upon Himself.

To take upon yourself the sins of others is essential.

Jesus says to His adversaries, 'Upon you may come all the righteous blood shed upon the earth, from the blood of righteous Abel . . .' (Matthew 23:35). Now, of one crime the Pharisees were surely not guilty. They had no part in the slaying of Abel. There were neither Jews, nor Pharisees at that time. How can Jesus call them to account for the blood of Abel? Why does Jesus in the same discourse say, 'O Jerusalem, Jerusalem, thou that killest the prophets . . .'? (Matthew 23:37). Nowhere is it written in the Bible that any prophet had been killed in Jerusalem. Neither does profane history report such a happening.

There *is* sense in it. Who does not learn to consider the guilt of others, of people completely foreign to him, even people belonging to past generations, as his own, will never be able to grasp deeply as his own the righteousness of somebody else.

If I don't learn to see myself in every other man, if I cannot identify myself with Cain, the murderer of thousands of years ago, and see my hands stained with the blood shed by him, how will I grasp deeply that

Jesus is my real self and that His sacrifice, which also happened a long time ago, is my righteousness, how will I learn this identification with Christ?

It is the daily practice of Christians wherever they meet sin and crime to appropriate them, to feel them as their own.

I was able to show that man when he quietened down that Christ had besmeared Himself with mire, that He allowed Himself to be treated as dung, to expiate even the crime of torturing fellow-Christians. To think that I will be able to see in heaven as a beautiful, glorious saint, clothed in white, the man who had felt this mad impulse to throw himself into excrement, this is really exhilarating.

But let us not deceive ourselves. Cases of remorse and the recovering of Christians who have gone to the extreme of torturing their fellow-Christians, and this in the service of atheists, have been extremely rare. In ninety-nine per cent of these cases their hearts were hardened for ever. Who knows if there does not exist a point beyond possibility of return?

Just study *Psychopolitics*, the book of Lavrentii Beria, former Minister of Interior Affairs of the Soviet Union, and you will see how scientifically the Communists have thought all this out.

Lenin had passed nights with Professor Pavlov to learn how his experiments of forming conditioned reflexes in dogs could be applied to men. They *can* be applied. Men, like dogs, can be brought to what is called, in reflexeology, ultra-paradoxical behaviour, to lick the hand of the one who beats him, and to bite the hand of the one who feeds him. Necessary for this are nervous exhaustion through sleeplessness, lack of food, humiliations, refined tortures, prolonged detention in darkness, or with a blinding light, etc. With men, one thing more had to be added in order to obtain perfect results. The cruelties must be inflicted by those whom you love most and in whom you trusted.

Those who have not studied Pavlov, and the Soviet policy based on his theories, or have not experienced them personally, will always be dupes of the Communists. Metropolitan Manuil Lemeshevski of Russia spent twenty-seven years in prison. After this, he broke down. He became a member of the Soviet-controlled Orthodox hierarchy whose work consists in serving and flattering the regime which had made him suffer so cruelly.

Monsignor Augustin, the real head of the Roman Catholic Church in Romania, has passed through prisons. I was with him. His love and faith shone until a certain moment. Then he cracked. Can the Communists now rely fully on him?

It is interesting to see with what confidence the Romanian Communists have sent Orthodox priests, who have been in jail together with me, who have been beaten, treated with electric shocks, sentenced to long terms, to carry on propaganda in the U.S.A. and in France. They now travel around the world praising the liberties under Communism. They don't defect. By the Pavlovian system they have been changed into neurotics with ultra-paradoxical behaviour. Their reaction to the stick is no longer abhorrence, but loyalty. They are faithful to those who have beaten them. At a certain stage, those who are made to drink urine in prison would no more recoil from it, but beg during the night, 'Give me more urine.' A Romanian Orthodox priest, Anania, who has suffered much in Communist prisons, now in the U.S.A., is loyal to the Red-controlled Patriarchy.

This belongs to the world of madness, but it is a madness scientifically produced and maintained.

A Western church leader has before him some Russian or Romanian Baptist or Orthodox leader. He is fully assured that this man has many years of Communist prison behind him. How can this Westerner be convinced that this man is not a reliable Christian, but a lackey of Communism? First of all he would have to study reflexeology and Communist psychopolitics. But what Western Church leader has studied Communism? In what seminaries is it taught under this aspect, even though Communism rules one-third of the world?

To whom should we tell that young men trained to become officers of the Secret Police have to desecrate in an obscene manner the image of the Holy Virgin? It makes them ruthless torturers of Christians.

I was told that a Western publisher would never publish such gruesome things, and that Westerners would not read it. Well, we will have to circulate this information in handwriting, as the Bible circulates in handwriting in Russia. But the Christians of the free world must know all these things, and in detail, because it might be their future fate. I will not tailor what I have to say, I will not trim my thought in order to ensure it will be published.

From hundreds of prisoners in Piteshti, some detained there for their Christian beliefs, others for patriotic activities, three succeeded in committing suicide. Two kept their faith undefiled. All the others denied their beliefs, divulged secrets, denounced even their parents, became, in their turn, torturers of other prisoners. The experiment has succeeded.

Ceausescu and Kosygin and Tito and Ulbricht know now how to do it. Blasts with nuclear power have been made. Today, the big powers only stockpile nuclear bombs. But they are piled for the purpose of using them in the future. The same is true here. A terrific experiment has been made in Romania, unequalled in this history of tortures. It was not made only by the late Prime Minister Gheorghiu-Dej, who has died. The rest of the gang collaborated with him. The method was also exported to Red China. Today, Romanian Communists wish to trade with the West. They want loans, so they behave themselves for a time. But their character has remained the same. They have never given up Leninism. Their aim is still the uprooting of religion. And at the moment which they consider convenient, the Romanian and other Communists will begin again with the sure methods of Piteshti.

Romania an example of *liberalised* Communism? The very poor Romanian Christians were authorised by the Government to gather a sum which was huge for them and to build a Baptist church in the town of Dej. At the inaugural service, a great crowd filled the church. Indignant about this, the Communists ordered its closure. During three days and nights the Christians watched around their church to hinder its being torn down. Then the police came with dogs and dispersed the Christians. The church was destroyed by bulldozers.

As regards the liberalisation in Romania, it is more important to know what Romanians think, not casual visitors who do not know the truth. I will tell you the situation in the form of a joke which circulates widely in my country: a tourist calls to a taxi-driver, 'Are you free?'; he answers, 'No, sir, I'm a Romanian.'

And a second joke. Ceausescu went to inspect an asylum for madmen. These were instructed to shout 'Hurrah'; Ceausescu was very pleased, but he observed that one of them present did not cheer him. He asked that man why. The man answered, 'Comrade Ceausescu, I am not mad. I am a doctor.'

CHAPTER 11

Beauty Shines at Midnight

God needs children to worship Him by deeds. *Nauka i Religia* of January 1971 tells the story of a child who, contradicted by many of her class, asserted boldly that God exists. It was in a school in Gorki, a town in the Soviet Union. To stand up for God means to risk losing mother and father. Christian parents are often deprived of their children if these witness to their faith in school. In the end a girl proposed: 'Let us make an experiment. We will bury a cross, the symbol which is holy for you Christians, as you say that Christ died on it for our salvation. If nothing happens, there is no God. If there is, God will punish me.' Christ's child continued quietly to assert that God is. She knew that God can vindicate His Name. The girl who had mocked buried the cross. After a few days, her mother died suddenly. It was a sign from God for the whole class. The fact was rumoured in the whole town. And even the main magazine for spreading atheism had to publish an account of it in order to explain it away.

A courier of the Christian missions to the Communist world reports: 'I saw a wife of a Christian martyr in Romania. He had left many children behind. She looked amazingly young, though she had grown-up boys. I expressed my amazement. She answered, "Suffering has renewed my youth." '

Another Christian told him, 'We would like an easing of our conditions but not the full ceasing of oppression. We fear that liberty would make us lose our burning love.' Yet another, 'We, when we think of the cloud of witnesses in the spiritual skies (Hebrews 12:1), are happy that the part of the sky which is most cloudy is over the Communist countries. We are glad to give the greatest number of confessors and martyrs.'

The Romanian Churches all know what has happened in Piteshti. They know that in the future excess of torture might break them, too. But as long as it has not happened they speak out for the Lord.

An eye-witness at the trial of the Seventh Day Adventist pastor Boian told us what happened. The judge asked Boian, 'Do you believe that Jesus will return and destroy His enemies?' 'He surely will.' – 'Will He destroy me also?' 'Without the slightest doubt, if you do not repent.' – 'Do you regret to have preached illegally?' 'I have done what was pleasing to the Lord. As for you, God will punish you here and in eternity.' 'You were not allowed to preach.' – 'God not only allowed it, but commanded me to preach. Read yourself the order in the Bible. It is in Matthew 28.'

He was sentenced to eight years' imprisonment. This happened in 1969, in the liberalised Romania of Ceausescu. I had been in prison with the same Boian in 1964. At that time he was sentenced for only three years. Romania had not been liberalised then!

We have news that important leaders of the Communist Party listen to Christian broadcasting and are greatly impressed by it.

Our brethren in Romania allow themselves jokes. I

was at the end of a conference with church leaders belonging to the World Council. Their aim had been to convince me about the liberties in Romania. Some of them were Lutherans and they were not aware that for twenty-five years the Romanian Lutherans were not allowed to publish one issue of a religious magazine. But one of the leaders handed me a letter. It was in Romanion. A Romanian Christian had asked him to smuggle this letter out and give it to me, which he did. In the letter our Romanian brother ridiculed the naïvety of this very church leader who had expressed to him his enthusiasm about the huge attendance in the Romanian-speaking Protestant Churches. 'Your churches are so over-crowded,' he said with excitement. 'There are people sitting on the floor, on the windows, standing crammed.' He did not wonder why it was so. It is wrong that a church should be over-crowded. The normal thing is to have as many churches as are needed to give people the opportunity to worship in comfortable conditions. It did not even pass through the mind of this church leader that Christians had walked forty miles and had arrived seven to eight hours before the meeting started to be sure to have a sitting-place.

He would not believe what the writer of the letter had told him that two thirds of the Romanian-speaking Protestant assemblies were closed. It could not be true. The important leader from the West had spoken himself with the butcher Dogaru, head of the Communist Departments of Cults and with the official Baptist leaders. They had assured him that there is full religious liberty. 'Should I not believe such a high official and a leader of a Baptist Union?'

God mocked him by making him bring out the letter in which his own unfitness for his high position in the Church was made clear.

But in this same letter, our brother told us about a meeting of pastors, at which the Commissioner of the Communist Government was present, who complained that since the Red rule the number of believers has increased by three hundred per cent. 'We, the authorities, do not wish this to happen, and will give you no increase of liberty.' Some official church leaders congratulated the commissioner and assured him that they would obey all the rules of the Communists and do nothing that would bring about a further increase in the number of Christians. In any case, their numbers increase in spite of and not because of these leaders.

The letter finishes by telling us that Jesus had been tempted with words of Scripture. The Christian leaders in Communist countries are also tempted by Bible verses. Foremost among these is Romans 13: 'Let every soul be subject unto the higher powers', forgetting that this chapter describes the legitimate ruler. He is a minister of God for the good and an executor of wrath upon him who does evil. If a ruler rewards evil and punishes good, it is not about him this chapter speaks, and to him we owe rebellion, not subjection.

Ah, and what about those hundred thousand Bibles printed in Romania? I am still waiting for someone to come forward and assert that some team from the West has counted 100,000 Bibles and has seen to the distribution of 100,000, no more and no less. The assertion of Communists has been believed. Any cashier who issued a receipt for £100,000 without having counted the money would be fired.

Good news from the Soviet Union, too. A Communist newspaper, of the 12th of December 1970 complains that the choral club of the Collective in one village simply changed and became a church choir. It has eighty members. But more than that!

The Soviet Union had the first strike for God! In a village in Bielorussia, Zarechanka, the Communists closed a church and turned it into a grain store. The whole village refused to work for several days in protest. From the nearby town of Grodno, students were brought to milk the cows and do other work. But the students joined with the strikers! The report about this was published in *Chronicle of Current Events*, No. 16/71, an underground magazine of Russia; this has existed for many years, being protected by hidden accomplices in the Secret Police!

The president of the Soviet Regional, Molotchko, was compelled to order the cleansing of the church from the grain, to return its property, to repair the damaged building and to punish those who had closed the church.

No! the Christians of Russia are not wearied or worn out, neither by the tyrants nor by their accomplices of modernist Western theology! They are strengthened by the knowledge that they are not alone in their fight. Let our solidarity strengthen their hand for the fight.

Praise God that, while workers in Britain, Sweden, Italy and Australia strike, being duped by godless Communists who wish to enthrone atheism in their countries, the Soviet Union had the first strike in history proclaimed to the glory of God!

CHAPTER 12

Persecutions of Christians in Africa

When I wrote *Tortured for Christ* and *The Soviet Saints* there was still something like an Iron and Bamboo Curtain. Since then these have ceased to exist. Communism no longer begins somewhere in the Berlin Wall and terminates in North Korea. Three countries of Africa—Guinea, Zanzibar and Congo Brazzaville, have become avowedly Communistic. Syria and Iraq are Sovietised! There are Communist guerrilla fights in many parts of Africa. Moscow-and-Peking-instructed Arab guerrillas fight believing that they do it for their national cause. But Communists are not so unselfish as to train guerrillas for something which will benefit an ideal other than their own. The Reds have made great advances in Laos, too.

I am sorry that lack of space does not permit me to give details about other European and Asian Communist countries, but I wish to write a few words about Africa.

The hammer and hoe is now on the flag of Congo-Brazzaville (the sickle is unknown there). At the first governmental rally in Brazzaville, 'The Internationale' was sung as the national anthem. Christians still remember the cruelties of the Sambis who had killed a multitude of missionaries and native Christians just a few years ago. Now the murderers rule the country.

Let us remember just a few of the crimes committed by those who rule this part of the Congo today. They opened the chests of living men, tore out their hearts, and ate them. They cut off the ears and genitals of native Christians and compelled them afterwards to eat their own organs. They opened forcibly the mouths of Christians and poured benzine into their bellies; afterwards, they split open the bellies and set fire to the benzine. (From the book of the Rev. W. Van Straaten, *Where God Weeps*.) Those who committed these crimes were Chinese-Russian-Cuban-trained guerrillas. They have conquered the leadership of the country now.

The W.C.C. has decided recently to give money to Communist guerrillas in Africa. We will exemplify by one case who these guerrillas are. The A.P.I.G.G.C. (African Party for the Independence of Guinea and Green Cape) is backed by the Communist dictator of Guinea, Sekou Toure. These guerrillas fight to unite all Guinea under his rule. Let us have a look at what kind of freedom these guerrillas fight for.

President Sekou Toure said to his National Assembly of the 18th of January 1971: 'Let the people slaughter, cut into pieces and burn their enemies wherever they find them.' (*The Guardian of Liberty*, February 1971.) Toure has sentenced ninety-two persons to death. Conacry Radio announced on the 25th of January 1971: 'The verdict delivered yesterday at the stadium in Conacry was greeted by an explosion of popular rejoicing . . . this reached its culminating point this morning at the sight of the bodies of the hanged . . . the grisly sight of the bodies of those individuals resulted in a veritable carnival. Men, women, children and old people expressed their great enthusiasm as well as their indignation. They spat on the bodies of those hanged.'

The Roman Catholic archbishop of Conacry, Raymond Marie Tchimindo, was sentenced to hard labour for life. He allegedly died in prison. Brother Hermann Seibold, who worked in Guinea for the German Christian Youth Village Organisation, was beaten to death.

It would be useful specially for American Christians to think over the fact that in the United States, Communism can rule only in the form of Black Power, and that such treatments will be applied to American Christians if ever the country falls under Communist rule.

Odinga in Kenya has allowed his house to become a meeting place for all leftist sympathisers, for Communist diplomats, and for all who wanted the victory of the Red Star. Communist friends gave Odinga money to send students to universities in the Red Camp. A coup from his side has been prevented at the last moment by Kenyatta, as has been prevented that by another Communist-paid adventurer in Lesotho.

Seventy tons of atheist literature are brought into Africa from Red China every month. But it is not only the thoughts of Mao which are used to attract people. The Communists attract youth in Southern Africa by sex demonstrations of black and white nude parties.

At Nambuanfongo and Luvo, in the Portuguese territories, Communist guerrillas trained in China, Cuba and the Soviet Union have bound Christians, and others who dared to oppose them, to long boards, and fed them through rotary saws like trussed-up logs of wood. One of the criminals, describing afterwards the events to a reporter of the Paris newspaper *Le Monde*, said with a broad smile, that once the Christians have been bound, 'We sawed them lengthwise.' Christian women, black and white, were raped before and after they were split open. Some were raped, still alive, with their entrails dragging to the ground. They stuffed the vitals into the mouths of those who had dared to keep their own faith and would not accept cruelty as a religion. Al Venter, a journalist of remarkable objectivity, says in his book *The Terror Fighters*: 'The incidents as described here were not isolated.'

Blood and tears — this is the story of Communism everywhere.

CHAPTER 13

*The Attitude of the Church of the Free
World Towards Communism*

In Italy every third man votes for the Communists, in
France every fourth man. Even Christians vote un-
knowingly for those who will torture them when they
come to power. Communists are masters of deceit. They
assure everyone in the West that they will give religious
liberty. But this is what Lenin promised also in Russia.
To promise costs nothing. Italy and France have had
already the rehearsals of revolution. Christians who
sympathise with Communism would do well to ponder
the following quotation from *Voprosi Filosofii*, a Moscow magazine, of January 1968, 'From the point of
view of Marxism-Leninism, freedom of conscience demands full denial of religion, its definitive defeat and
its exclusion from social life.'

In the United States, revolutionism has taken an
extremely subtle form. Be it enough to quote from *Do
It*, the book of Jerry Rubin, a leftist leader: 'We've
combined youth, music, sex, drugs and rebellion with
treason—and that's a combination hard to beat.' This
man has been freed by a court of appeal, being con-

sidered as not dangerous. Bombings and killings of policemen and occupation of campus buildings or churches are daily happenings.

Should all this make us become anti-Communist? What will we have gained by this? Hitler was surely an anti-Communist. Notwithstanding, he was a tyrant and a rogue. In my eyes, to be an anti-Communist means just nothing. I am much more interested to know what a man is for than what he is against.

The Communists are men, and must be loved.

I am against any compromise with *Communism*, because it always starts from lies. The Evangelical Relief Committee for interned persons of the German Lutheran Church and the Department of External Affairs of the same, denied in 1969 the existence of Christian prisoners in the Communist camps. This, contrary to obvious evidence. The policy is not to upset the Reds.

About cases of sentencing to death Christians in the Soviet Union under trumped-up charges of ritual murder (Krivolapov, Smirnovia, Losko), we appealed to the Pope and to the Protestant leaders, and to the World Council of Churches. *Nobody said a word in protest.* Nobody asked us even for the cuttings of the Soviet Press itself, bringing these accusations. Why? Ask your bishops, priests, ministers, evangelists and pastors.

All such compromises disarm the Christian fighters who have to oppose Communism. The *Journal of the Moscow Patriarchate* No. 3/68 reports on a symposium of church leaders in East Germany. Buievski, foreign secretary of the Moscow Patriarchate, stated there, 'The fifty years since the October revolution characterise a new Socialist society as serving peace and love of mankind . . . Every Christian must accept the fact that the foundation of the Communist revolution is love of

mankind and he must thank God for the revolution.'
Those attending swallowed these infamies. Buievski's
boss, Khrushchev, had told mankind how many innocent victims were killed by Stalin in this revolution
for which we are called to thank God. Stalin's own
daughter gave other facts.

I don't believe in what is usually called anti-Communism, and I refuse to join any anti-Communist
organisation, but neither do I believe in compromising
with Communism in the religious or in the political
sphere. Every bridge built towards Communism will
make it easier for the Reds to cross rivers and oceans
to destroy freedom.

Communism is a religion of hatred. I believe in what
St. John of the Cross taught, 'Where there is no love,
put love and love will spring up.' I believe that it is
right to follow the example of St. Patrick who, after
having been held as a slave by the Irish, and treated as
slaves were treated at that time, when he escaped to
England, prepared himself for a noble mission. Passing
over many hindrances, he went back to his former slave-
holders and brought them to Christ.

Psalm 104:35 is inexactly translated. In Hebrew
the words are: 'Let the sins (not the sinners) be consumed out of the earth and let the wicked be no more.'
The Talmud comments: 'When the sins disappear,
there will be no more sinners.'

It is written in Proverbs 24:29, 'Say not, I will do so
to him as he hath done to me: I will render to the man
according to his work.' When you tread a flower under
your feet, she rewards you by giving you her perfume.

Christians are on the side of people oppressed by the
Communists. Their duty is to help them and their
churches by providing them with Bibles and Christian
literature, by broadcasting to them the Gospel, by send-

ing relief to the innumerable families of Christian martyrs.

Christians are on the side of the Underground Church in Communist countries, not on the side of the official church leaders there, who have become stooges of the Communists. The Communists are anti-man, something similar to what anti-matter is in the physical realm. If anybody makes friendships with them and obeys them now, what will be their attitude when the Anti-Christ appears?

Therefore, when the Baptist World Alliance had convened a Congress with 10,000 in attendance in Tokyo, I was there and shouted the cry of the sorrows of the persecuted Christians in the Soviet Union. I protested against the parading of the Red flag of Communism at a Christian Congress, though it is stained with the blood of martyrs. All flags were paraded there, except the Israeli and the Czech.

Pentecostals convened their own World Congress. My son and daughter-in-law unfurled there an inscription telling about Russia's jails, which are full of Christians. Many Christians, especially from the world leadership of the Pentecostals, do not cease to join together in solidarity. There was at this Congress a delegation of Communists saying that they represented hundreds of thousands of Pentecostals of the Soviet Union. *Freundschaft*, the German language Communist newspaper of the Soviet Union, of the 9th of December 1970, writes: 'In the district of Kirov there are cases where sects which are forbidden by our legislation hold their meetings secretly, trespassing against the law. These are sects like the Pentecostals.' So, the Pentecostals are a forbidden sect. Whom then did the 'official' representatives at the Pentecostal World Congress represent?

But by helping the Underground Church we embrace in our love its torturers, too. Our ministry must extend to them. They should also be won for Christ.

St. Patrick won Ireland. We wish to win the Communist world for Christ.

Every kind of missionary work in which the passion of Christ is passionately preached is valuable. But the missionary work in the Communist lands should have top priority. From the point of view of salvation, all men are equal, but it is not so from the point of view of current missionary strategy.

When St. Paul wrote that the gospel of Christ is the power of God unto every one that believes, to the Jews first and also to the Greeks (Romans 1 : 16), it was not because the salvation of the Jew would be more precious to God than that of a man of another nation. He speaks here from the point of view of the strategical priority. The most powerful arguments St. Paul had for his assertion that Jesus is Saviour, were the prophecies contained in the ancient Holy Scriptures of the Jews. A Gentile had to think it over well if he should become a Christian or not. To become a Christian could mean that he could be thrown to the wild beasts. Caution would counsel him first to ask some Jewish neighbour if the assertion of St. Paul regarding the contents of the Scriptures was true, since he, very often, would have no access to them. As a rule the Jews would answer, 'No, Jesus has been a deceiver'; in this way cancelling all the missionary efforts of the apostle. It was, therefore, of the utmost importance to preach the Gospel first to the Jews, to those depositories of the sacred scrolls, in order to have an impressive group of Hebrew Christians who would testify that their prophecies had been fulfilled in the person of Jesus. Then followed the possibility of winning those of other nations.

The same thing happens now. The salvation of an aboriginal in New Guinea or in South America is as important as that of a Russian. But if the aboriginal in the jungle remains unsaved, he cannot destroy the Church and Christian civilisation. If we do not bring salvation to the Communist world, the Communists can destroy these. Don't forget they have a piled-up experience of perfect torture. They can wipe out Christianity in a huge part of the world, as Mohammedanism wiped it out for centuries in North Africa, where it previously flourished. Gone then will be all missionary societies which spread the Gospel among primitive peoples. Gone, too, will be most of the church life in the free world as well.

The Times, London, of May 1968 announced that Russian nuclear-power submarines continuously patrol the Atlantic and Pacific coasts of the U.S.A. They have submarines containing sixteen missiles each with a range of 2,000 miles and they are patrolling at only eighty miles distance. Should we react to the ravages which they can inflict with retaliatory nuclear ravages?

What about winning the crews of such Soviet submarines for Christ? What about winning the Communist world, oppressors and slaves? Once converted, Communists would never destroy our cities, which they will know to be full of churches and believing souls. I understand, surely, by the word conversion something entirely different from the phenomenon usually called so, which did not stop Christians of different nations killing each other with the benediction of their priests and pastors in two world wars. I mean by conversion a new birth, becoming a new creature, embracing all men in the love of God.

This is our attitude towards Communism—neither hatred nor compromise, but soul-winning love.

Will we succeed in winning the Communist world? Surely, under two conditions:

(1) We must be able to answer the questions of the Communists and the objections they raise against our religion. This means a huge intellectual task to which the best heads of the church must dedicate themselves.

(2) We ourselves should live up to the standard of what we teach. We do not demand the impossible. 'Be ye perfect', or 'Love with all your heart' are commandments which cannot be fulfilled all at once. But it is the same as the conquest of a country in war. You have a strategy for attaining the final aim. And you have daily tactical decisions for each step forward towards the goal. The standards of Jesus are the final end to be attained. Demanded from us is only the daily step forward in this direction. Neither God nor men can ask us more than this. But we will never win the Communist world without such decided steps. Winning the Communist world for Christ is therefore connected with an urgent Christian revolution in the free world.

Our love extends surely also to anti-Communists, to whom we show a new constructive way. It extends also to those who compromise. We have full understanding of the religious leaders of the West who do so. Eighty-five per cent of the Orthodox of the world and two-thirds of the European Baptists live in Communist lands. To break relationship with their official leaders means to be left with very little.

But why should they forget completely the persecuted Christians? The Baptist Underground Church of the Soviet Union addressed a communication to the President of the World Baptist Alliance who had visited the U.S.S.R. They wrote: 'One might have expected that you would have visited at least one of the persecuted Churches, or would have expressed the desire to meet one of the believers who had recently been imprisoned. . . However, your visit was to the All-Union Council of Evangelical-Christian/Baptists, a State show window for religious freedom. . . From the height of a royal visit it is of course difficult to notice the tears of orphans and Christian widows.' St. Athanasius preferred to remain alone with the truth, having against him a whole ecumenical council, which expelled him under no less slanderous accusations than the killing of a bishop and the raping of a virgin.

Krasnov-Levitin, our greatly persecuted Russian brother, writes: 'Cowardice is the mother of all vices. Because of it, an honest man becomes a crook, a free man becomes a slave; a good man becomes a rogue.' Cowardice is cowardice even if you call it common sense, caution or circumspection. My doctrine knows none of these—but only one word, temerity.'

We can understand the Western church leaders and the reports they furnish, but we cannot approve of them. No compromise, but secret Christian missionary activity in the Red Camp, is our line.

CHAPTER 14

What We Should Not Do

Through letters or in big rallies with question and answer sessions, I have been asked again and again, 'What can we do to help our suffering brethren? What can we do to hinder the spread of Communism in the free world?'

Before answering the question 'What can we do?' I would say first what we should not do.

Don't remain asleep. The Ukrainian writer Shevchenko wrote, 'It is terrible to fall in prison and chains, but it is much worse to sleep in liberty.' Your country and your Church is also a target of world-Communism. They work already at the subversion of your country and they wish to destroy your Church.

Free yourselves from illusions. Don't believe such general vulgar sentences as 'right triumphs in the end'. The end might be after centuries. Mohammedanism triumphed over Christianity in northern Africa a thousand years ago, and the situation has not been reversed until now. When Jesus promised that the gates of hell will not prevail against His Church, He relied on the fact that His disciples would not sleep, expecting victories to fall from heaven. Leave the beautiful looking but false sentence 'God will save us.' God does not help two and two make anything else but four. He will never make spiritual sleep and apathy give, as a result, Christian triumph. If we go on as until now, the persecution of Christians will become worse in Communist countries and Communism will expand further. The world in which we live is harsh and unromantic. Nice, hope-inspiring slogans do not prove true.

Do not see the main foe in Communism, without realising that we are its accomplices. The great hindrance to spreading the Gospel in Communist lands is not the Iron Curtain. We can easily break through that. The hindrance is the Silk Curtain of easy living. I saw in Miami an ocean show. A barefooted man fought with an alligator. He hit him with a stick on his head, he drew him by his tail. The alligator snapped occasionally at him, but never did him any harm. I asked the man, 'You seem healthy. You can make your living in some other manner. One day the alligator will bite you and you will be gone.' He answered, 'Out of the question.' Marvelling about his assurance, I asked him if he had an agreement with the alligator. He said, 'No, but before every show the alligator is over-fed. An over-fed alligator does not bite.' This is the situation of many Christians in the free world. The U.S.A. spends more money on chewing-gum than it gives to missions.

When I preached about these things in the West, many Christians told me, 'You are right.' This is not enough. Take the decision. What useless or even useful things do you renounce in order to be able to do more for the holy cause?

A church with comfortable pews, with philosophical sermons which you can enjoy, a church without missionary endeavour, but debating trifles, while humanity is engaged in a race with catastrophe, can become the Judas Iscariot of Christianity. THE CHURCH, the Bride of Christ, is undefiled, unpolluted. She will never betray. The churches—Roman Catholic, Anglican, Orthodox, Lutheran, Baptist, Pentecostal—are human institutions. They have played many ugly roles in past times. Remember the Inquisition, the anti-Semitism, the connivance with Hitler, the splits in matters in which nobody knows the real truth, the blasphemous heresies. These churches can betray again if they do not watch.

Opinions differ about the much-debated Baptist Church in Moscow. Is she genuine or not? Apply the test: on what unevangelised field does it do a missionary work? Well, she has accepted not to do missionary work even within the Soviet Union. A Church without missionary work is no Church. The persecuted Church under the Roman emperors sent missionaries to countries far away. The official Baptist Church in Moscow has no mission—no secret mission, if no open mission is allowed. By this simple fact, she has stepped out of the rank of Churches.

But what about our Churches? Christian missions are on the decrease. There are fewer Protestant missionaries than ten years ago, and these at the ratio of five women for one man. The population of the world grows by sixty-three millions a year. Only two millions will have a chance of hearing the gospel.

Fight Communism, but don't be arrogant towards it. Communism has not the monopoly of evil. There are shortcomings in Christianity, too. We are forgetful of the needs of the world we are commissioned to save.

Beware of anti-Communist hysteria or bigotry which makes you suspect a Soviet spy in everyone who speaks out for the poor, the hungry, for those who are victims of racial, national or religious discrimination. Communism thrives on the injustices of our society.

Don't hope that politicians will solve the Communist problem. Churchill wrote, 'It is the duty of a civilised world to conquer Russia. The Soviets do not represent Russia. They represent an international concept, entirely foreign and even hostile to what we call civilisation.' But it was he who had given at Yalta half of Europe into the hands of the Communist butchers. Richard Nixon wrote in *Reader's Digest* of September 1961, 'The U.S.A. goal must be nothing less than to bring freedom to the Communist world.' When he became President of the United States, he danced with the Communist Prime Minister of Romania, Ceausescu, on a public square.

I don't think that the Communist threat will be abolished by military means. Neither do I wish it. We don't know much about life after death. But by killing a Communist I might deprive him of all opportunity of being saved. Soldiers are right to kill in legitimate defence of their country, but the aim must always be peace, a peace based on righteousness.

The whole military fight against Communism is dubious. If anyone should have a Vietcong flag in South Vietnam, an American soldier would shoot him. But thousands parade with Vietcong flags in the U.S.A. itself. Nobody bothers them. Americans don't fight Communism in Cuba. They don't fight it at home, but fight it in Vietnam, while making friendship with the Soviets who support the Vietcong. The political and military fight is led without decision to conquer and therefore could not succeed. No hope from this side!

CHAPTER 15

What Can Be Done?

Humans do not have the habit of committing suicide for another's grief, but that is exactly what we demand from you: 'To deny yourself, to die for yourself and to live for Christ, who is in grief and suffers again in his mystical body, to feel every pain of his holy martyrs as your own, to remember those in bonds as bound with them' (Hebrews 13:3). At this moment you have brothers and sisters kept in chains tied behind their backs, sometimes for weeks, having to lap their food like dogs. You have brethren and sisters in strait-jackets and gagged. At this moment, Mrs. Malozemlova weeps in her home. Seven children have been taken away from her, because she had taught them about God. And her children and the children of the family Sloboda and thousands of others weep, crying desperately, 'Mummy, Mummy.' They will not see their mothers again. At this moment in Red China Christians have their eyes gouged out, their tongues cut off. Die to yourself and live their life.

A Christian, even if he is well-to-do, free, young, healthy, is like his Master — always a Man of Sorrows, acquainted with grief (Isaiah 53:3). This because, like a sponge, he sucks in the sorrows of every innocent person, and shares them.

Share our griefs, help us to bear our heavy cross, as Simon of Cyrene helped Christ to carry his—this is the appeal of the Underground Church.

You hear again and again in churches, 'Crucified under Pontius Pilate.' Two thousand years have passed. The stain has not been washed away. Will it not some day be said that Christians in Communist countries suffered persecution, were without a Gospel, that families of Christian martyrs hungered, while Christians of the free world were richer than ever before?

Your riches, even if they are relative, will be a terrible burden to you at the last judgement. So will be, even more than your riches, your comfort, your easy-going, pleasure-loving ways. Unburden yourselves, prepare yourselves for meeting Jesus, who will tell you, 'I was in jail.' You seek His fellowship. Be in jail with Him. It is the only place where you can be with Him. He has never said that He will be in cathedrals.

Pray for the Underground Church. Elijah was a man with the same weaknesses as ours, but the fate of a country depended upon the prayers of this one man. Pray, having the same consciousness. The Christians of the Underground in Russia have organised a chain of prayer. They pray uninterruptedly twenty-four hours a day for the Christians in the free world. Do the same. Pray yourself. Organise prayer groups. Ask from your pastor or priest that there should be public prayer for the martyrs in Communist countries at every religious service. An old canon of an ecumenical council says that every liturgy at which the martyrs are not mentioned is not valid. Don't mention only the martyrs of centuries ago. Mention those killed today by the Communists.

And when you pray, be careful to do it as many prayer-books righteously say, 'together with the angels and archangels.' Everyone of us has a guardian angel. These angels have wings. Why? Because they wish to be our messengers. We have left them unemployed. Tell your angel: 'The Berlin wall and the Iron Curtain are not too high for you. Fly over them to a Christian in chains, to a mother deprived of her children, to a brother who passes through tortures and tell them that they are not forgotten, that somebody prays for them. Strengthen them in their faith.'

Don't simply pray, but agonise in prayer as Epaphroditus, yes, as Jesus Himself did.

Prevailing prayer is united with regular fasting. The Underground Church of the Soviet Union fasts on Fridays. They fast even in slave labour-camps, where they are hungry the whole week long. The Church Fathers and the great Evangelists believed in fasting. Tertullian wrote a treatise on this subject. St. Polycarp saw in fasting a powerful aid against temptation. Luther, Calvin, Spurgeon, the Catholics until not long ago, all stressed the necessity of fasting.

The thousands of Christians in Red prisons have no Communion Service. Remember them at every Communion. When you hear the words, 'This is my body broken for you', remember the body of our Lord broken on Golgotha, but remember also His mystical body, broken by Communists today. Not only was His blood shed, His bride's blood is also shed on many modern Golgothas. Have a tear for those who give their body and blood today. Don't eat the wafer just as cattle eat grass.

When I came to the West, and afterwards to Australasia and Africa, bringing the message of the Underground Church, when my books *Tortured for Christ*,

The Soviet Saints and *In God's Underground* appeared, the response of Christians was huge. The books were translated in a total of twenty-three languages. And in nineteen countries of the free world, missions to the Communist world were created.

The purpose of these missions, which collaborate in an international fellowship, is to help the Underground Churches in Communist countries with Bibles and Christian literature, with Gospel broadcasts, with relief for underground pastors and families of Christian martyrs, as well as to spread the Gospel among the revolutionaries in the free world. An ounce of prevention is better than a pound of cure. It is better to prevent Communist revolutions by winning leftish youth for Christ, than to help the persecuted Christians after Communism has won.

Spurgeon said once, 'I would be missionary-minded just for selfish reasons. What a joy it will be, when I enter into heaven and find some souls saved through my efforts or prayers or gifts. They will come and say, "We are here because of your missionary interest and efforts." '

Not many Christians have this holy selfishness. They make concrete plans for going to church or to a movie, they make concrete preparations for going on vacation. They don't make detailed preparation for their going to heaven.

Every time we take a breath, four souls pass away. Every hour 4,000 men die. It is 100,000 a day. One third of these live under Communist rule, prevented by force from hearing the Gospel.

Leave aside discussions regarding post- or pre- or a-millennialism, leave aside debating infant or believers' baptism, apostolic succession, quarrels about the interpretation of the Bible (which was not inspired by God so as to become subject for debate), leave aside the stupid modern theologies of whatever kind. Theology is sin. It produces only quarrelling. If the carpenter Jesus tried to read the books of Karl Barth, Bultmann, John Robinson and others like them, or those of their theological opponents, He would put them aside after the first pages. He would not understand them. They are much too cleverly written. Believe in God, in love, in eternal life and tell the story of Jesus to lost souls.

Don't expect your church leaders to do it. It was rarely they who started it. The Bible Society was started when a girl from a Welsh farm met one faithful pastor. The China Inland Mission was started by an employee in a drug-store. The pioneer of Protestant missions in India was a cobbler, Carey. Moody was a salesman of shoes. Spurgeon never went to college. Up, cobblers, salesmen, men of little culture, men without degrees but with ardent love toward Christ! You do the work! Many pastors and bishops join you. Welcome them when they do. But don't wait. The Lord's work is urgent.

CHAPTER 16

The Need for Literature

Pravda of August 1969 states that one quarter of all the literature produced on the whole earth is produced in the Soviet Union (which has less than one tenth of the world's population).

Christians believe the Word to be God and yet do so little in the matter of literature. The most widely-translated book in the world is no longer the Bible, but Lenin's writings. It has had 968 new translations since 1946, the Bible has had only 887.

The world is simply flooded with the book of Mao Tse Tung.

In the Communist world, Bibles and other Christian literature are very scarce. A Communist book *Children and Religion* by Ogrizko, tells how parents in the Soviet Union feed their children with the Word of God. The Party has published *The Comical Bible*, a book ridiculing the word of God, but which contains excerpts from the Holy Scriptures. The Christians glue paper over all the mocking words, leaving only the Bible verse and feed thus the souls of their children. In the same way they also use other atheistic books.

The underground printing-presses work. Much literature is smuggled in. Yet how vast is the need still unmet! There are in the Soviet Union alone some 220 million inhabitants with a hunger for the word of God unknown in the West. We simply must give them more literature!

We find no difficulty in doing so in the Far East. Literature is flown in by balloons from South Korea.

We have broken also through the Iron Curtain.

Let us listen to what the Communists have to say about this. *Leningradskaia Pravda* of the 12th of October 1967, writes about 'a stream of religious literature and leaflets directed towards our country.' In the article we are told that the literature is spread by Christians who come disguised as tourists. In other articles they complain that it is smuggled into sacks or bales of various goods imported into the Soviet Union. The Moscow magazine *Voprosi Filosofii* No. 6 of 1967 enumerated among the causes of the persistence of religion in the U.S.S.R., 'the distribution of literature . . . which comes from abroad.' At the big trial of Soviet writers, Galanskov was accused of having met a foreigner, who introduced herself under the nickname Nadia, in the monastery Troitsa Sergheievska. Nadia had brought religious literature from abroad to Galanskov.

The Moscow magazine *Agitator* tells us the story in its issues 2/70 and 2/71: 'There are anti-Soviet personalities who practise the launching of balloons with anti-Soviet contents. Sometimes they use the following means; they throw bottles with anti-Soviet literature into the sea. They count on the fact that the currents will bring them to the shores of Socialist countries. On one occasion the first and fourth pages of Soviet newspapers were copied exactly, and on the second and third pages were printed articles and notes anti-Soviet in aim. Such newspapers were sent to the U.S.S.R. under the form of 'returns' from capitalist countries, the person being 'unknown at this address'. Our foes put their material also in the covers of magazines and books published abroad by leftist organisations. The enemies of Socialism are shrewd and skilful.'

So as to be very sure of what kind of material this anti-Soviet literature is, the *Agitator* tells us the results of such activities.

'Lastly, an activity of different religious sects which are fanatic and don't fulfil the Soviet laws, has been observed. The members of the sect of Evangelical Baptist Christians founded by Prokofiev, for example, teach the refusal of participation in social life, the trespassing against the law regarding religious cults. They strive to impart to children their religious views and morals which are foreign to Soviet men.'

The Soviet newspaper *Kazakhstanskaia Pravda* of the 16th of June 1971, writes that the brethren in the Soviet Union print great quantities of Christian literature themselves.

Sister Vershtshaghina from Alma-Ata, the couple Ivan and Maria Pavliutchenko, Valentina Maximova and Tamara Sokova are under arrest because they arranged for the printing of thousands of Christian hymnbooks in a printing shop belonging to the Soviet state, with the connivance of the Director, and of all the workers and drivers. Nobody denounced. So much is

Christianity sympathised with by the average Soviet citizen, even if he does not appertain to an Underground Church.

The Underground Church of the Soviet Union has just released information that it has created a publishing house called *The Christian*, where 40,000 gospels and hymnals have already been printed. It has informed even the Soviet Government about the fact, the respective letter surely bearing no signatures! They risk their lives for spreading the Word of God. And should we be reluctant to spread a book or a newsletter telling about their heroism?

You can help so that Communist countries will have Bibles and Christian literature.

In the Chinese town of Chungking, Bibles, hymnals and prayerbooks were burned publicly, the Christians being compelled to attend. One of them profited from the momentary inattention of Red Guards to snatch just one page which had not been consumed by fire. He had to act quickly and could not get more than one page. For years the Underground Church of this town has fed upon this single page of Scripture.

I wondered which page it was. It could have been a page from Genesis or Nehemiah, full of genealogies, which have their importance, but which they would not have understood. I expect to see in heaven the angel of the church in Chungking and to congratulate him for the skill wherewith he directed the hand of that Christian towards the right page. Because after two years of striving, I have succeeded in getting the information as to which page they have.

Every Sunday they read, 'On this rock will I build my church; and' neither Mao Tse Tung, nor the burying alive of Christians, nor the gouging out of eyes, nor the cutting of tongues, nor the desecration of church buildings, nor 'the gates of hell shall prevail against it' (Matthew 16:18). They have the page with this text. Really something to live on.

But it is a righteous thing to give them more of the Bible so that they may learn new things about the Person who builds the Church, about hell and heaven.

CHAPTER 17

Broadcasting the Gospel

The Communist customs officers cannot prevent streams of Christian literature from entering Communist countries, but they still make the work difficult and dangerous. Secret printing-presses are sometimes discovered, and this leads to arrests.

The Communists have no customs officers in the air. The radio-waves arrive. In Red China death sentences have been passed upon some for listening to Gospel broadcasts from abroad. But still they listen. In the Soviet Union they have jamming stations, but these are very expensive. The territory of U.S.S.R. is huge. There are large portions of this country where the radio is well heard. In the European satellite countries the messages are clearly heard.

The radio work is most effective. We know of Communist members of governments and diplomats who listen regularly to them. We know cases of conversion among them as the result of this broadcasting of the Gospel.

A young Chinese smuggled out a letter in which he said that he had been an atheist. But once he saw in a movie-picture a lady wearing a cross. He inquired what the cross meant and was told that it is the symbol of Christianity. But he could not find out what Christianity meant. There were no Christians in his area. By chance, he tuned in to a Gospel transmission. He listened to one broadcast after another and began to love Christ. He asked, 'Does God accept somebody from Red China? You have mentioned the church several times in your sermons. But with us it is not so. God is in heaven, we are in Red China, and we have no church in between. All the churches have been closed. How can we enter heaven?' The poor lad did not know that he has many churches. The whole Church universal is his. Then he puts a second question, 'How should I pray? You always finish by prayer. I don't know how to pray.' But then he says what he imagines prayer to be, and gives the most beautiful definition of it which, to my knowledge, has ever been given—'Prayer means to speak the whole day so as to be able to say after every talk, "Amen".' I think we must all learn from this definition. You cannot well say 'Amen' after having quarrelled with your wife.

We possess letters from Russia of men converted by radio transmissions, though they have never seen a Bible in their lives.

New congregations are created in this manner. I quote a letter from Romania: 'We wish you to know that in the last three months over fifty souls in our village have been converted, listening to the radio. Among them the wife of the head of police. In this village there were no believers before. Now they all listen to the word of God. Work. Work as much as possible and God will reward you.'

The missions to the Communist world broadcast the Gospel in the languages used in the various Communist countries.

The Underground Church of the Soviet Union has also secret radio stations of its own. The authorities have been aware of such activities for some years now. Drastic sentences, even death sentences, were given to those found out. It did not help. The Underground Church organises new short-wave radio stations instead of the older ones employed. Christians are aware that they risk death. But it is the leaders of the Underground Church who know the mentality and the language of their people best who speak to souls.

The Communist authorities are alarmed, which shows that our brethren are on the right track. 'Novoe R. Slovo' of the 21st of December 1970 writes about 'religious programmes' spread over such radio stations.

I think this work strikes a deadly blow at all those who have contested the very existence of an Underground Church.

The spiritual level of the preachers of the Underground Church, who have suffered prison and tortures, is higher than ours. We must help the Underground Church to develop on a great scale this radio work of its own.

Your support in Bibles, literature and radio makes the Underground Church in the Soviet Union grow. *Kazakhstanskaia Pravda* of the 15th of December 1970, writes that in the town of Balchash it had been considered until recently that there were no believers in medical institutions. But now an enquiry has been made, and many of the doctors and nurses declared themselves to be Orthodox, Old Ritual Orthodox, Catholics, Lutherans, Baptists, etc. Bibles and the radio sponsored by you through our Organisation have achieved this.

CHAPTER 18

*Help to Underground Pastors and Families
of Christian Martyrs*

The Christians in Communist countries are poor, they
have to pay heavy fines. They have difficulty in supporting their pastors. Here help is required.

Innumerable Christians are in Communist prisons.
Marchenko, a prisoner in a Soviet camp, has written
the renowned book, *My Testimony*. In it he says that in
nearly every cell he met some believers. How many
prison cells does the Soviet Union have? And what
about other Red countries? The families of martyrs and
confessors of the faith are hungry.

It is not easy to help them. Not so much because of
the Communists watching. We have learned to work so
that they do not know what we do. But we find resistance within the families of Christian martyrs, themselves. One sister whose husband is in prison said, 'Why
do you wish to deprive us of the privilege of bearing a
heavy cross? Why do you wish to separate us from our
loveliest friend, sister poverty?' Russian Christians have
inquired if they could not help their Western brethren
financially. Seeing that in the fifty years of Communist

dominion the Western Christians have done nothing to help the sufferers our Russian brothers, who could not imagine that we are indifferent to their fate, have drawn the conclusion that we are very poor in the West. They thought about helping us!

We overcome the resistance and help the families. From one we received a beautiful letter of thanks. She is the mother of nine children. Her husband is sentenced to ten years: 'I thank God for the privilege he has given me to bear a chip of the cross of Christ. My small children ask me when Daddy will return. But Daddy has put his life at stake for the faith once for all delivered to the saints. When the Communists took my husband, they mocked us, saying, "Now let your God come and help you. You will see that you will starve." But love has a long arm. It stretched out to us a piece of bread from far away and now the Communists are ashamed.'

We have succeeded in bringing food and clothes into Siberian slave-labour camps and in getting letters of thankfulness from there.

'I thank God for the privilege to bear a chip of the cross of Christ.' Only a chip, so little is it to have a husband in prison and nine children to care for! I have heard somebody complaining in the West about a heavy cross that he had to bear with having to buy a cheaper car rather than a more luxurious one.

Those who have eaten excrement and drunk urine because they believed in the same Lord, have the right to receive from the Christians of the free world a piece of bread. Even a piece of chocolate would not be too much for them.

The Teaching of the Twelve Apostles, an early Christian book, says, 'A prophet who asks money is a false prophet.' This applies also to missionary organisations. I personally would never give to an organisation which demands money. Its cause must be so luminous that people should ask the organisation to accept its gifts.

It is ugly for preachers to speak about the verse, 'Set your affections on things above', and then to fuss because the mission income is not high enough. It is higher than that of the first band of apostles.

My duty as a teacher in Israel is only to convey to you what has been always and everywhere the doctrine of Christianity in this matter. St. Ambrose said, 'If my brother hungers and I do not help him, I am a thief. And if my brother dies of hunger, I am a murderer, too.' I have seen many Christian prisoners literally starving from hunger.

The words, 'I have been young and now am old; yet have I not seen the righteous forsaken, nor his seed begging bread' (Psalm 37: 25), hold true only where a David is king. Under the Communists, children of righteous fighters for the faith eat sometimes from the garbage. They have to be helped. Ask your church to do it, by whatever means she will know best.

Soviet Lithuania of the 4th of June 1967 stated that the Easter collection at the Kaunas Orthodox Cathedral was 1,274 roubles. This is approximately the salary for a year of a Soviet factory-worker. In the West we are far from this. *Questions of Scientific Atheism* of May 1968, tells that in a village in which, according to their description, the average church attendance is about 300 persons, the income of the church has doubled in one year. The latest report about yearly income was of 23,000 roubles. Thus a churchgoer in an official village church gives on the average eighty roubles per year, which is one and a half times the monthly salary of a worker on a collective farm.

I don't ask you for money for a certain mission. I

don't ask you for money at all. I have described to you the Christian life of the Underground fighters. It is of such a beauty that you have to go immediately to your pastors and friends to find out to what extent you and your church can have the privilege of sharing the sufferings and future glory of the elect among the elect.

CHAPTER 19

*Answer to the Most Frequent
Criticisms*

We don't pay much attention to criticisms. We have found that, as a rule, those who criticise our activity never care to help persecuted Christians. Those who help never criticise. I, personally, do not care what the whole world thinks of me. It did not think highly of Jesus.

The official All-Union Council of the Evangelical Baptist Churches of the Soviet Union (a bunch of Communist agents) has published a brochure in English, which they give out to English-speaking tourists visiting the church in Moscow. On page 54, they assert that 'the rumours about the persecution of our church and about the alleged physical destruction of believers are in contradiction to reality.' After having said this lie, they single out Pastor Wurmbrand for attack, saying that 'his activity is very far removed from preaching the true gospel of God.' They know who works effectively in the Soviet Union. They know which organisation to attack. Their insults are a compliment for our Mission. They are those who denounce our brethren to the Secret Police, in order to get them arrested.

Gerhard Simon in *The Churches in Russia* (publishing House, Manz, Germany): 'The manifestations of Wurmbrand are determined by high emotions; they are without compromise and often naive... His judgments about church politics prove a terrifying narrowness... The danger of Wurmbrand's grotesque distortions consists in the fact that he calls Christian groups in Eastern Europe to resistance until death.'

The W.C.C. criticised U.S.A. Congressman Rarick in a fourteen-page letter for having taken the defence of Christian martyrs in the Congressional Record, based on the information of our Mission.

They write: 'In the present Communist regime, strong powers for the humanisation of society lie hidden ... Wurmbrand becomes really dangerous.'

All these remain without answer.

But I would wish to answer some sincere doubts about our work.

There are some Christians who ask, 'Don't you endanger even more the persecuted Christians by your secret work of smuggling in Bibles and relief, by supporting the whole underground movement?'

We, surely, could endanger them. Did Jesus endanger men by exhorting them to become His disciples? He says, 'I send you forth as sheep in the midst of wolves' (Matthew 10 : 16). This surely was to endanger lives. The apostles would not have died a premature martyr-death if Jesus had not called them to such a risky task. St. Paul endangered the life of his converts. Listening to him, led to their being thrown before wild beasts. Every Christian soldier must be ready to die for his Lord. Every officer in the Christian army must be ready not only to die, but also to send others to death for the good cause. If the Reformers had not preached their doctrines, thousands would not have been burnt at the stake. Neither would Catholics have died, killed by the Protestants, if the Pope had not taught them to withstand what he considered to be a heresy. If you are convinced that your cause is the cause of Christ, it is right to give your own life and to teach others to do the same.

In the end, it is very dangerous to feed a starving man. You might spoil his stomach. Should we, therefore, not give food to the hungry? No, they should be fed, but with caution. So, the underground work must be done, though it is dangerous, but avoiding blunders and wrong methods.

A Hungarian Christian wrote an article against me, in which he says that by my activity I am fixing the noose of the rope wherewith the Christians in Communist countries will be hanged. This was in 1967. Time enough. Not only was not a single Christian in Hungary hanged or even imprisoned because of our activity, but the contrary happened. At this moment, not a single Protestant Christian is in prison for his faith in Hungary. Neither was anyone jailed because of our activity in any other Communist country. We know how to work cautiously.

If the figures of those arrested in the Communist camp after the publishing of my book had increased, the guilt would have been put on me, but since I published it the Bible Society received permission to print Bibles in some Communist countries. The merit is not attributed to me!

I am criticised for being an anti-Communist. I will answer with a word of Spurgeon, 'We cannot do otherwise than contend with those who contend with God.'

Lenin wrote: 'All modern religion and churches are agencies of bourgeois reaction, which serve to protect exploitation and benumb the working class.' The Leninists desire the destruction of the Christian religion. This is their plan and it must be defeated. We have to fight against Communism. Christianity has always fought against its foes. Never has the Church canonised any leader who has compromised with the enemy, only those who stood up against him. Those whom we call saints, far from bearing tyrannies quietly, went rather in the opposite direction. The gentle St. Bernard of Clairvaux wrote, 'The Christian glorifies in the death of an infidel, because Christ is thus glorified,' and Anselm of Canterbury, referring to the crusaders, said, 'Our men, returning in victories and bearing many heads, fixed upon spikes, furnished a joyful spectacle to the people of God.' If there is a general consensus in Christianity to call men who have spoken like this about the adversaries of Christianity, 'saints', why should I criticise who say much less? My message is: 'Expose the evil of Communism, defeat it, but glory in converting the Communists, not in having killed them.'

Everyone honours Dietrich Bonhoeffer, martyred for Christ, who justified under the Nazis the murder of the tyrant. Why then should I be criticised as deploying an unjustified anti-Communism because I exhort Christians, 'Win the tyrants for Christ.'

Dear brethren criticised me for not preaching the pure Gospel.

My Gospel is full of the tears and blood and spittle and excrements and urine which sully the faces of the saints of God in Communist countries. It is a dirty Gospel. A Gospel which hides these ferocities committed against Christians, which does not call us to fight for freedom and righteousness, to sympathy and sharing with sufferers, is not a Gospel at all.

Neither do I know any one important preacher in the history of the Church who should have preached the so-called pure Gospel.

John Chrysostom has also been charged with not sticking to the Gospel, because he said in his sermons that the Archbishop Theophilus of Alexandria was guilty of simony, of misappropriating funds and practising brutality. This saint raged against degenerate Eudoxia, Empress of Byzantium, calling her a second Jezebel. He had to go into exile for this. Was he wrong? Was St. Ambrose wrong not to allow the king to enter the church when he returned from an unjust war?

Why did Charles Spurgeon not stick to the pure Gospel? It was the time of the war of secession. And Spurgeon spoke out on the side of the Northern Confederation which fought for the abolishment of slavery in the Southern States. His books, yes, and he himself in effigy were burned in the Southern States by his fellow-Baptists. He did not restrict himself to preach only the personal salvation of souls.

From these preachers I have learned which is the true Gospel.

I am criticised for my strong attitude against the Orthodox Metropolitans and Protestant leaders in the Red camp who flatter the Communists.

How many truths exist? When Hitler invaded Norway, the Lutheran Archbishop Berggrav refused any compromise with him. He preferred to become a prisoner. Nearly unanimously, his pastors followed his example. This was, probably, right. But Romania, Bulgaria, the Baltic countries, Hungary and Czechoslovakia have been invaded by Soviets. I expect the world church leaders to tell me that Berggrav was wrong. Then I would understand. They greatly honour his attitude as right, but at the same time put in the leadership of the

World Council of Churches the bishops and Protestant leaders of Russia, the Balticum, of Romania, Czechoslovakia and so on, who flatter the oppressors of their native countries.

Pope Pius XII and the leaders of the German Lutheran Church of that time, are criticised for not having taken up the defence of the Jews against Hitler. But the Jews were driven out of Poland and are discriminated against in the Soviet Union today. The very existence of the state of Israel is put under a question mark because of the Soviets. Do the official leaders of the churches in the Soviet Union take up the defence of the chosen people? Has the World Council of Churches done it?

Hitler had invaded Czechoslovakia. It was a shame that the church leaders of Germany at that time had not protested. With this everyone would agree. But Czechoslovakia has been invaded again by the Soviets. Did the official church leaders of the Soviet Union protest? The underground fighter, Krasnov-Levitin, protested publicly and was sentenced to seven years' imprisonment for this. Who represents the conscience of Christ in Russia today?

Others tell me, 'Whatever you say about Communism may be right. But we should first put in order Christianity's house.' It is like saying that every policeman must first be born again and become a saint before he gets a right to fight the gangsters. Christianity may have many shortcomings and failures. But it has the truth about Christ and about eternal life. The Church has a divine and human side. The divine side is constituted by the word of God, the sacraments, the fellowship with angels and the glorified saints, the Lordship of Christ, the beautiful examples of those who follow Him in truth. The Church has also a human side. It is constituted of sinners who can and do commit bad deeds. Communism has no divine side. It is not even human. It is anti-human. Communists don't persecute only Christians, they just hate. They hate each other. The Communist Kosygin hates the Communist Dubcek, the Communist Mao hates the Communist Kosygin, comrade Brezhnev hates comrade Tito, Stalin killed his nearest friends and Khrushchev kept his own wife in prison for eight years. In opposing Communism the Church is right, even as the unconverted policeman is right when he fights a gangster.

Christians should simultaneously put their own house in order and fight Communism.

'But,' I am told, 'there is surely something valuable in the work of the legal Churches. The activity of your mission meant a death-blow to the legal work.' It did not. On the contrary, we helped it. Pastor Paul Hansson, secretary of the Lutheran World Federation, declared in *Kristteligt Dagbladet*, Copenhagen, that they could help legally the official churches in Communist countries with four and a half million crowns, more than in previous years.

I will mention one more objection: 'The church has its leaders, its Presidents of Protestant Unions, moderators or bishops. We have to listen to them. Some of these do not agree with you. Should we not rather listen to our bishops than to you who are not a bishop or hold no other high position in the church hierarchy?'

My answer may seem histrionic, but it will be, 'Ask that a bishopric should be given to me.' How is it that Wurmbrand who has brought the message of the suffering Church in one third of the world has not yet been made a bishop or leader of some other Protestant denomination? That he does not belong to that denomination does not count. St. Ambrosius was made bishop before even being baptised. Neither did he have a D.D. He had only a commission from God for the Church. It is not my fault that the Underground Church is not considered and that its messengers are not received in high places. Milan Haimovici, the greatest hero of the Christian fight in Romania, a man who has suffered beyond human imagination and always maintained the highest standards, though an ordained Lutheran pastor and one of the greatest preachers in Romania, works now as caretaker of a church in Western Germany. They had no place for him. He does not mind it. Violets enjoy the shadow. Neither do I care for high positions in the church. But I had to give this answer for those to whom church authority is everything. Not every Church leader is a child of God.

When two Church leaders wrote circular letters against me, one in U.S.A., the other in West Germany, I remembered that a fourteenth-century Catholic historian wrote about Wycliff, 'That instrument of the devil, that enemy of the Church, that author of confusion to the common people, that image of hypocrites, that idol of heretics, that author of schisms, that sore of hatred, that coiner of lies, being struck with a horrible judgement of God, was smitten with palsy and continued to live till St. Sylvester's day, on which he breathed out his malicious spirit into the abodes of darkness.' Excommunicated after death, Wycliff's skeleton was exhumed and cast away.

There are many faithful bishops and other Church leaders who have supported us.

To summarise, all the well-meant criticisms have two common denominators: critics consider Church life as they know it in the free world as being the normal. The Underground Church with its devices, nicknames, passwords, meetings in the wood, non-submission to state laws, infiltration into Communist ranks, they see as a Church gone wrong instead of seeing it as an entirely new phenomenon. It is the Church of the catacombs adjusted to conditions of the twentieth century, which has a perfected police, but also a perfected conspiratorial technique.

Others cannot find a label for me. They do not know in what frame to put me. I enter no fixed set of rules. Every order of monks has its rules. So has any Protestant missionary society. But according to what rules did St. Francis Xavier, the first missionary to India, work, or, later on Hudson Taylor, Carey, Morrison, Patton, Livingstone? They established rules for those who would come after them. Until then they were rules unto themselves, as it always is with pioneers, with spearheads. I do not compare myself with these great personalities, but on my modest level I am also a forerunner, the first to bring to the Western Evangelicals the message of the Underground Church. Neither did I have a predecessor to set me rules when I started the secret missionary work in the Soviet Army. I can be judged according to nobody's rules. If your country should be taken over by the Communists and you are forced to work underground, you will have to do it according to the rules learned from me.

There have been personal attacks against me — 'madman, demon-possessed, Nazi, Facist, anti-Semite, Communist, Anarchist, Jesuit agent, illiterate, fake, racketeer, etc.' The slanders have never amounted to what has been said against those who shine today as beautiful stars in the spiritual sky. If these had to endure much worse than me, why should I, an unworthy servant of the Lord, defend my person?

But I do defend the cause of the Underground

Church. What I assert about its sufferings and victories is unchallengeable. This fact makes opponents try to side-track Christians from the message to the messenger. They would like people to discuss, 'Who is Wurmbrand?' instead of 'What is the Underground Church?' They will not succeed. The cause of the Underground Church has already become the cause of faithful Christians all over the free world. In one country of the free world after another, missions are formed to support it. Christ is on our side. We will win. Making no apologies to the critics, we go brazenly ahead, burning the candles at both ends.

I know very well that I am one-sided. There exists a holy one-sidedness. When the Jews were burned by the Nazis, a man had to be one-sided. It would have been wrong to put the questions: But have Jews never sinned against the German people? Have not some Jews done very wrong things in the time of the Weimar Republic? Was it absolutely wrong for Hitler to rebel, asking for more vital space when Britain had a world-wide empire, and Russia had a huge territory badly managed, and so on? Men, even children were burned. They had to be defended. All other things did not count. One-sidedness was the right attitude.

The Underground Church is not ideal. It has its sins, as has the legal Church in Communist countries. But it is persecuted. This obliges me to be on the side of the underground fighters. The Talmud says: 'If an unrighteous man persecutes a righteous, God is on the side of the persecuted righteous. If a righteous man persecutes an unrighteous, God is on the side of the unrighteous. God is always on the side of the persecuted.'

But taking decidedly the part of only one side, I don't have the deceptive certitudes which usually accompany one-sidedness. There exists no face without a back, no reality without a counter-reality. There is much to say for dialogue with the Communists. Contacts with the official Church are also very useful. And I ask all those in authority that this should continue, but never forgetting the brethren in chains.

CHAPTER 20

My Last Word

Many Christians of the free world, if they had lived in Noah's time, would have said, 'There are no signs of rain. It's just ridiculous to speak about the menace of a flood. Noah must be a right-wing crank who sees sinners under every bed. Why does he not keep to true religion, to the pure Gospel, instead of predicting an approaching geological catastrophe which is not his business? Geology does not belong to religion, neither do floods, but only the personal, individual salvation through the blood of the Messiah who will come one day. In any case, there is no hurry.' If they had lived in Noah's time they would have perished with the ungodly. The exceptions would have been few.

There are surely more signs of a Communist menace today than signs of a flood when Noah began to construct his ark. As for Noah's Gospel, he had it directly from God. God must have some idea as to which is the pure Gospel. And He instructs a teacher of righteousness not to stress for a while personal salvation, but to speak about geology and to make weather-predictions.

This because the catastrophe to follow was to be a punishment from God, just as is Communism.

We have more signs of approaching catastrophe than in Noah's time. John Kennedy has been killed by Moscow-trained Oswald, Robert Kennedy by Sirhan, who declared in his diary that Communism is the best system. There is hardly a day in the U.S.A. without Communist-inspired explosions, killing of policemen, riots, occupation of university buildings.

Gus Hall, the secretary of the Communist Party of America, then a little man, said some twenty years ago, 'I dream of the hour when the last congressman is strangled to death on the guts of the last preacher. And since the Christians seem to love to speak about the blood, why not give them a little of it? Slit the throats of their children and drag them over the mourner's bench and the pulpit and allow them to drown in their own blood and see whether they enjoy singing their hymns.' (Quoted from the Hearing of the U.S.A. Senate Sub-Committee 86th Congress, p. 798). But Hall has worked hard since and he has reached the point of declaring that Communists and liberal Christians share so many goals, that they can and should work together for the same thing. This same goal cannot be the victory of Christianity. Hall would not work for that. Then which is it? Should theologians and pastors have succeeded in preparing unconsciously the bloodbath against their brethren? Communists are now sometimes guest speakers at the principal services of churches in the U.S.A.

The influence of Communism in Italy and France has been already mentioned.

In Britain their influence is great in the trade unions. But not only there. The *Liverpool Daily Post* of the 29th of May 1968 reveals an admission of Sir Hugh Greene, then Director-General of the British Broadcasting

Corporation, that he has Communists on his staff, 'but they are none of his business'. They *are* the business of the listeners who can be brain-washed by disguised pro-Communism.

In all Arab countries, the trade-unions, the universities, the army, the police, and the Moslem brotherhoods are infiltrated by Communists.

According to *A.B.N.* of May 1969, the Kremlin finances its world-wide offensive as follows: Brazil, 40 millions a year, Argentina 30, Mexico 24, Chile 14, India 30, Indonesia 300. Apart from India, only Kerala gets a part of 66 millions, West Germany 60, Turkey 10 and so on.

In Japan, professors have committed suicide because of the Communist-inspired turmoil on the campuses, during which they have been compelled to confess publicly their crimes, exactly as in China.

We have shown the clouds of a near tempest in Africa.

By 1972 the Chinese Communists, who already have the nuclear bomb, will also have the missile to launch it and they are determined to do so. The Russian Communists have their orbital bomb. It may fly over your head as you read these lines. Treaties with them are of no value. They don't keep their promises.

Communism can be overcome. God has a chosen tool for this purpose. It is the Underground Church which gives to the peoples oppressed by the Communists the inspiration of the highest possible ideal — the service of Christ; the Underground which infiltrates even the high-ranking Communists and can win them for Christ.

I have before me a bunch of letters from Christian prisoners of the Soviet Union. They show us the quality of its fighters.

A few quotes from them. From one: 'Communists

have put on the wall of our cell a poster "Reason is against Religion". But weapons are used only against the living, never against the dead. So this poster told me that religion is alive, and I thanked God.' Another describes a scene from his trial. A Christian child was brought as witness for the prosecution against him. 'But our children are unafraid. When asked by the judge, "Who performs the baptisms?", the child answered, "This is an internal affair of the Christian Church. I can give you no information about it. The secrets of the Church are not for unbelievers. You first repent, then you'll have a right to know what happens in the Church." ' This child knew that by speaking thus he might be taken away for ever from Mummy and Daddy. But behind the Iron Curtain, Christ is loved in the only manner in which He should be loved, i.e. to the point of folly, and sacrifices do not count.

My son, Mihai, has also been brought up in the aura of arrests and trials. They were familiar to him.

In another letter from Soviet prisons we find Brother Alfred Boettcher's last word before the court: 'I have one aim in my life. This is to bring as many sinners as possible to Christ. Communists usually finish by putting in prison their own comrades. When you, Mr. Judge, sit on this form, remember my witness for Christ.'

The Underground Church fights for the salvation of souls. But like Noah, she does not remain in the sphere of pure religion. She is also a vanguard fighter for freeing the world from the Communist menace.

She is persecuted, but she can say the words addressed once by Theodor Beza to the king of Nevarra: 'Sire, it belongs in truth to the Church of God, in the name of which I speak, to receive blows and not to give them. But it will please your Majesty to remember that it is an anvil which has worn out many hammers.'

The Christians of the free world must support whole-heartedly the Underground Church or see in this generation their own Churches subverted and destroyed. This is the choice.

There is One greater than the Church. Its head, Jesus Christ, will pour out the spirit of grace upon His followers everywhere. Instead of useless talks about the merging of empty churches of different denominations in the West, there will be a real union of the free Church and the Church of martyrs.

One of our couriers writes: 'I recall the joy the sister in Russia had last night, when she saw the Russian Bibles on the table. She literally ran and kissed the stock of Bibles, then the husband, the wife and I gathered round the table and prayed. The next morning, the brother was up at five o'clock, wrapping them up to distribute them.' Such joy and love is contagious. From the Underground Church, the Western Christians will learn the enthusiasm, the ecstasy, the cherishing of the Word of God, and of the high calling to be a soldier in Christ's army, the divine impatience to see the Kingdom of God coming.

If my personal desire counted for anything, I would retire for quiet communion with God, as I had it in the solitary cell. But God decides. I can have communion with Him only to the diapason of the shrieks of my beaten and tortured brethren. My place is on the twentieth century's Golgotha.

Christ suffers here again in His mystical body.

On His right side suffers the penitent thief. The last words of Zinoviev, president of the Communist International, shot by Stalin, were, 'Listen, Israel, the Lord our God is one God'. The last words of Iagoda, head of Russia's Secret Police, were, 'There must be a God. He punishes my sins.' The last words of Yaroslavski, president of the International Organisation of the Godless, were, 'Please, burn all my books. Look, the Holy One. He has waited long for me. He is here.'

On the left side are the impenitent Communists. They have the deep suffering of a bitter heart.

Then there is the huge crowd of millions who just stand by and look upon what is happening, as at Golgotha. And you can hear from the bride's mouth the cry, echoing that wherewith Jesus died. To make you hear that cry was the purpose of this book. It is not so much a cry of suffering. This they have learned to bear. It is a cry of anguish for the multitudes of Communists and Communist-indoctrinated souls who cannot come to Christ because there is nobody to instruct them.

I would like to leave the work of supporting the Underground Church and go to theological universities, to pastors' studies, to Church leaders, and tell them, 'Just give up cutting the Bible asunder, your worthless theological debates, your endless and fruitless discussions about merging or not merging into nothingness.' Some call me mad. Then let mine be the frenzied cry of souls that go to hell in the Soviet camp, after having lived their whole earthly life in hell: 'It is because of your neglect. Don't you fear God? Don't you know that you will give account to Him?'

I can breathe not only gentle words, I can breathe also fire. If good words would not help, I would vituperate, just as Jesus did at times.

The Christians in Communist countries have endured prison without expecting any help from the West. They have kept the faith. To spread it to all creatures, as their all-embracing love commands, is not in their power without our help.

The souls who perish because of the Communist poison are an overwhelming sorrow, a painful wound on their soul and mine. Would you not try to heal this wound?

I have described atrocious sufferings through which Christians pass there. It was not to make you pity those hapless ones, but to pity those who have the opportunity to be useful, and do not take it, let alone the galleries of nonentities who quibble at this or that of my sayings. I am not infallible. Not everything that I say must be right. My character and my deeds are also far from perfect.

But that the Church of the free world must join hands with the Underground Church in the fight for Christ, against Communism, is surely right. This do, and God will bless you.

Inquiries and offers of help
may be sent to:
CHRISTIAN MISSION TO THE
COMMUNIST WORLD,
P.O. Box 19, Bromley, Kent, BR1 1DJ, England.